DWELLING IN HIS PRESENCE

DWELLING IN HIS PRESENCE

30 Days *of* Intimacy *with* God

Cynthia Heald

NAVPRESS

NAVPRESS

NavPress is the publishing ministry of The Navigators, an international Christian organization and leader in personal spiritual development. NavPress is committed to helping people grow spiritually and enjoy lives of meaning and hope through personal and group resources that are biblically rooted, culturally relevant, and highly practical.

For a free catalog go to www.NavPress.com
or call 1.800.366.7788 in the United States or 1.800.839.4769 in Canada.

ISBN-13: 978-1-61521-024-4

Cover design by Arvid Wallen
Cover image by Shutterstock

Most content was previously published in *In the Secret Place of the Most High* (Thomas Nelson, 2001).

Scripture quotations in this publication are taken from the *Holy Bible, New International Version* (NIV). Copyright © 1973, 1978, 1984 by International Bible Society. Used by permission of Zondervan. All rights reserved; the New American Standard Bible (NASB), Copyright © 1960, 1962, 1963, 1968, 1971, 1972, 1973, 1975, 1977, 1995 by The Lockman Foundation. Used by permission; *The New Testament in Modern English* (PH), J. B. Phillips Translator, © J. B. Phillips 1958, 1960, 1972, used by permission of Macmillan Publishing Company; THE MESSAGE (MSG). Copyright © 1993, 1994, 1995, 1996, 2000, 2001, 2002. Used by permission of NavPress Publishing Group; *The New English Bible* (NEB), © 1961, 1970, The Delegates of the Oxford University Press and The Syndics of the Cambridge University Press; the *Amplified Bible* (AMP), © The Lockman Foundation 1954, 1958, 1962, 1964, 1965, 1987; the New King James Version (NKJV). Copyright © 1982 by Thomas Nelson, Inc. Used by permission. All rights reserved; the *Holy Bible*, New Living Translation (NLT), copyright © 1996, 2004. Used by permission of Tyndale House Publishers, Inc., Wheaton, Illinois 60189. All rights reserved; *The Living Bible* (TLB), copyright © 1971, used by permission of Tyndale House Publishers, Inc., Wheaton, IL 60189, all rights reserved; and James Moffatt, *A New Translation of the Bible, Containing the Old and New Testaments*. New York: Doran, 1926. Revised edition, New York and London: Harper and Brothers, 1935. Reprinted, Grand Rapids: Kregel, 1995.

Printed in the United States of America

1 2 3 4 5 6 7 8 / 13 12 11 10 09

CONTENTS

Preface   7

The Father and the Child   9

1. Come and Talk with Me   11
2. Where Are You?   17
3. I Stand at the Door and Knock   22
4. Don't Be Afraid, for I Am with You   27
5. Blessed Are Those Who Trust in the Lord   33
6. I Know the Plans I Have for You   39
7. My Peace I Give to You   45
8. I Have Overcome the World   51
9. Store Your Treasures in Heaven   56
10. I Am the First and the Last   61
11. But on This One I Will Look   66
12. Your Names Are Written in Heaven   72
13. Shut the Door   77
14. Abide in My Word   82
15. The Truth Will Set You Free   87
16. Keep My Commandments   92
17. He Will Give You Another Counselor   98
18. But by My Spirit   104
19. Look for the Ancient Paths   110

20. Keep Them from the Evil One 116
21. Fear Only God 122
22. Do Not Fear the Reproach of Men 127
23. Love Me More Than . . . 132
24. Set Yourselves Apart to Be Holy 138
25. I Will Not Remember Your Sins 143
26. Forgive Those Who Sin Against You 149
27. Go and Be Reconciled 154
28. I Will Repay Those Who Deserve It 160
29. I Correct and Discipline 165
30. Follow Me 171

The Father and the Child 177
Notes 179
About the Author 185

PREFACE

A continual cry of my heart is that I might always be deepening my intimacy with the Lord. I do not want to become complacent, or even satisfied, in my current relationship with Him. I desire to keep growing in my love and knowledge of God — in essence, I thirst for His ongoing power and presence in my life.

Perhaps the Scripture that most beautifully describes this special closeness is Psalm 91:1 — "He who dwells in the secret place of the Most High shall abide under the shadow of the Almighty" (NKJV). As we live in close fellowship with the Lord, as we seek intimate communion with the Most High, we will experience His power and Spirit. As we draw near to Him, children thirsting for His love, He will admit us to His secret place — a special residence of refuge and protection, of revelations concerning His ways and His character.

Dwelling together requires commitment, trust, and love from both parties. If I am living in another's home, then I need to abide by the host's wishes for how I conduct myself. If I seek a dwelling place with the Lord, then I must know what He desires of me.

As I began my quest of finding out what God might desire, I decided to consider the words that the Lord Himself might speak to His children. This book explores thirty phrases spoken directly by either the Father or Jesus. Some of these words are comforting, some stern, but all are from the heart of God, spoken clearly and lovingly for our good. If we listen and respond, we will be drawn into His presence.

As you read each chapter and reflect on the questions that follow, listen to these words of God and meditate on them as if He is speaking just to you, His beloved child with whom He longs to dwell. Your wholehearted response to His words will enable you to receive the power He imparts and the presence He extends. How it pleases our Lord when His children thirst for intimacy and righteousness! Jesus promised that those who hunger and thirst for righteousness shall be filled. My prayer is that through these words from God you will be filled, challenged, and inspired to dwell continuously in His presence. May you declare with the psalmist, "You will show me the way of life, granting me the joy of your presence and the pleasures of living with you forever" (Psalm 16:11, NLT).

God's invitation for deeper intimacy is echoed throughout all of Scripture. The particular passages in this book are only a sampling — but they have spoken powerfully to my heart over the years, convincing me that there is no other place I would rather be than dwelling in His presence.

Love in Christ,
Cynthia Heald

THE FATHER AND THE CHILD

The Child spoke:

Father, I thirst for Your power and presence.

Then come and dwell in My secret place.

Where is Your secret place, and how can I dwell there?

My secret place is close to My heart — you will find it by living
in constant communion with Me.

How can I live in constant communion with You?

By listening to My words and obeying Me.

Sometimes it is hard for me to listen and harder still to obey.

When you abide in My secret place, I have your undivided
attention. Then you can hear My words with a pure heart,
and I can impart My Spirit to strengthen your obedience.

Then I want to dwell in Your secret place. What shall I bring?

You need only bring My Book and an undivided heart
committed to love and follow Me.

I am ready, Father.

Good, I am pleased to have you close to Me, My child, so that I
can fill your heart and life with My presence and power.

COME AND TALK WITH ME

My heart has heard you say, "Come and talk with me, O my people." And my heart responds, "Lord, I am coming."

— PSALM 27:8, TLB

I had a young friend I really cared about; she was special to me and I wanted to encourage her by taking her to lunch and giving her a gift. When I called with an invitation, she was not home, so I left a message asking her to call me back.

Several weeks went by with no response. Every once in a while I'd think of her and wonder when we might be able to get together. Finally, we saw each other at church. I was delighted to see her and after a hug, I asked, "Did you get my message?"

"Yes, I did," she said, "but I've been really busy and just haven't been able to return the call."

I assured her I still wanted to see her and asked her to let me know when she was available.

Afterward, I thought of Psalm 27:8 where God "calls" with an invitation: "Come and talk with me, O my people" (TLB). Just as I wanted to spend time with my friend, the Lord wants to spend time with us. His invitation, though, encompasses much more than lunch; His offer includes a special kind of fellowship. The psalmist wrote in Psalm 91:1,

> You who sit down in the High God's presence,
> spend the night in Shaddai's shadow,
> Say this: "GOD, you're my refuge. I trust in you and I'm
>   safe!" (MSG)

Other translations tell us,

> He who dwells in the secret place of the Most High
> Shall abide under the shadow of the Almighty. (NKJV)

To *dwell* means "to remain, to abide, to stay." It conveys a constancy and a continuity — a daily, moment-by-moment communion with our Lord as if we are sitting down in His presence.

This is the relationship Jesus wanted with His followers. Andrew was a disciple of John the Baptist when John told him Jesus was the Lamb of God. Andrew and another man immediately began walking along behind Jesus. When Jesus asked what they wanted, Andrew replied by asking, "Rabbi . . . , where are you staying?" The Lord's response was, "Come and see." These men went with Jesus to where He was staying and remained with Him the rest of the day (John 1:38-39, NLT). A little time later, Jesus called the two sets of brothers who were fishermen (Andrew and his brother Peter, along with John and James) to be His disciples by saying, "Come, follow me, and I will show you how to fish for people" (Matthew 4:19, NLT). In both instances, Jesus invited these men into a close, intimate relationship with Himself. He wanted to spend time with them; He wanted them to have personal knowledge of who He was; He wanted to be deeply involved in their lives.

Just as the Lord opened His heart and life to the disciples, He wants to be intimate with all who love Him and are called by His name. To us Jesus says,

> Are you tired? Worn out? Burned out on religion? Come to me. Get away with me and you'll recover your life. I'll show you how to take a real rest. Walk with me and work with me — watch how I do it. Learn the unforced rhythms of grace. I won't lay anything heavy or ill-fitting on you. Keep company with me and you'll learn to live freely and lightly. (Matthew 11:28-30, MSG)

The Lord desires and invites us to walk with Him, to keep company with Him, to stay with Him. In the Upper Room Jesus gave a beautiful illustration of this intimacy: "I am the vine, you are the branches; he who *abides* in Me and I in him, he bears much fruit, for apart from Me you can do nothing" (John 15:5, NASB, emphasis added). Here Jesus gives the picture of a branch "dwelling" in the vine.

For me, to dwell or abide in the Lord's presence means taking the time to nurture my relationship with Him. Dwelling is responding to His call to come and talk by spending special time with Him daily, reading and studying His Word. It is planning mornings or days alone with Him. It is sharing my thoughts with Him throughout the day and listening for His thoughts for me. It is meditating on His Scriptures so I can know Him better. It is seeking intimacy on the deepest level.

This relationship meets our hearts' inmost needs for fellowship, acceptance, and for a place of safety and rest. This consistent dwelling produces the fruit of Christlikeness for we are abiding in the vine.

The opportunity to dwell in His presence should humble us and stir our hearts to answer this invitation at any cost. This intimacy was all that the psalmist David desired:

> One thing I have asked from the LORD, that I shall seek:
> That I may dwell in the house of the LORD all the days of my life,
> To behold the beauty of the LORD
> And to meditate in His temple. (Psalm 27:4, NASB)

David not only answered the Lord by saying, "I am coming," he also chose to make dwelling with the Lord the "one thing" that really mattered. God's offer to dwell with Him and talk with Him is ongoing and renewed day by day. It is our choice, though, whether we will respond to His gracious call.

Because of my friend's busy schedule, she was unable to respond immediately to my invitation. We eventually did have lunch, but I was somewhat disappointed that we could not have gotten together sooner. I wanted to know what had been going on in her life and I had a little something special to give to her.

Could the Lord possibly be "somewhat disappointed" when we allow a multitude of distractions to keep us from responding to His invitation? Yet we are the ones who deny ourselves the joy of His fellowship, and the gift of His love calls for us to come and talk with Him. Let us not keep Him waiting.

LISTENING TO THE MOST HIGH

Paul's purpose was to know Christ Jesus. Using his words in Philippians 3:7-8 as a guide, write out your desire to be intimate with the Lord.

EXPERIENCING HIS POWER AND PRESENCE

How does God's invitation to intimacy stir your heart?

What are some hindrances or distractions that keep you from consistently dwelling in His presence? Thank the Lord for His desire for intimacy and ask Him to help you always respond, "Lord, I am coming."

You did well to come; you do better to abide. Who would, after seeking the King's palace, be content to stand in the door, when he is invited in to dwell in the King's presence, and share with Him in all the glory of His royal life? Oh, let us enter in and abide and enjoy to the full all the rich supply His wondrous love hath prepared for us![1]

— *Andrew Murray*

Dear Lord, I am humbled by Your invitation for intimacy. May I not be content just to stand in the door; I desire to enter in and stay in order to enjoy the richness of Your grace and love. *Amen.*

WHERE ARE YOU?

*When the cool evening breezes were blowing, the man
and his wife heard the LORD God walking about in the
garden. So they hid from the LORD God among the trees.
Then the LORD God called to the man, "Where are you?"*

— GENESIS 3:8-9, NLT

"Mimi, I'm going to hide in the closet, and you come find me!"
Our grandson, Hamilton, loves to play hide-and-seek. As he listens to me call out his name and exclaim over how I can't find
him, his anticipation that he will soon be found causes him to
laugh out loud. As my calls get closer, he screams with excitement because he knows that a fun session of tickling and hugging is the reward when I discover him in his hiding place. We
have spent many hours playing this game with our children and
grandchildren. It is a blessing to know that someone who loves
you is seeking to find you.

There have been times, though, in our child-raising years

that our young children might "disappear," because they were doing something and they didn't want to be discovered. Years ago I recall a time of looking for one of our children. After futile attempts of calling his name, I began my hunt throughout the house, and I ultimately found him in the closet with a forbidden bag of chocolate-chip cookies! He knew that he was guilty, and the first thing he thought to do was to hide and hope that he would not be found. As a parent, I called and looked for him out of my love and concern for my child. It is no less so with our heavenly Father.

God's children, Adam and Eve, were lovingly created and placed in a picturesque garden where all their needs would be met. There had only been one parental warning — "You may freely eat the fruit of every tree in the garden — except the tree of the knowledge of good and evil. If you eat its fruit, you are sure to die" (Genesis 2:16-17, NLT). But the fruit was exceptionally tantalizing on this tree of good and evil, and the enemy of our souls, Satan, was present to cast doubt on their Father's word and to tempt them to disobey His command. As soon as they ate the forbidden fruit, Adam and Eve were as "wise" as God in knowing good and evil.

Before eating, this original husband and wife were naked before one another in freedom and purity. After yielding to temptation, their eyes were opened to sin and evil. Now in humiliation and defeat, for the first time in their relationship, they looked at each other and were embarrassed. Once they were innocent, now defiled. Once guileless, now guilty. Once unworldly, now worldly. Once trustful, now doubtful. Once obedient, now disobedient. Once shameless, now ashamed. How they must have thought, *What have we done? What has happened to us? What is this strange, uncomfortable feeling that makes us see each other and want to cover ourselves?*

It is from these catastrophic circumstances that the first instance of "hide-and-seek" is recorded. These children heard their Father enter the Garden. Guilty, afraid, and fearful, they hid themselves. Their Father called out, "Adam, where are you?"

I would think that in the past, Adam and Eve were always out in the open, waiting for their Father — longing for His communion and fellowship. Now they did something that they had never done before; they ran away from Him into the trees, hoping that they would not be found. How the sound of His voice must have pierced their hearts, for they knew that it was a call of a loving Father concerned about His children. He knew of their sin. He knew where they were! He wanted Adam to answer. He wanted to confront them and correct them so that they would not spend the rest of their lives separated from His presence.

In His relentless, passionate pursuit of His own, God continually calls out, "Where are you?" With this monumental question He is saying to us, "I love you. I care about where you are. I want to find you and be with you." If the Lord didn't want to interact with His children, He would ignore us. Our hiding does not prevent Him from calling out to us, for He seeks us willingly — desiring our fellowship, desiring to bring us out of darkness into His light, out of the trees into freedom, out of guilt into forgiveness.

In spiritual hide-and-seek, God never hides — He always seeks. He takes the initiative to find us, to call us to Himself, to be our Father. Once we respond to His call, then we no longer have to hide — in fact, we *can't* hide any longer! Listen to King David:

> I can never escape from your Spirit!
>> I can never get away from your presence! . . .
> I could ask the darkness to hide me
>> and the light around me to become night —
>> but even in darkness I cannot hide from you.
>> (Psalm 139:7,11-12, NLT)

Where are you today — are you in hiding? Do you need reassurance that your Father seeks you in love because He wants to restore you? Where are you today — are you so busy that you keep responding to His call by saying, "Not today — maybe tomorrow"? Where are you — are you thirsting for His presence and power, so that there is no need for Him to call your name in order to get your attention?

Listen to the Lord's question: "Where are you?" Let these precious, loving words draw you closer to the heart of the God who seeks you and wants you to dwell with Him in the secret place of the Most High.

LISTENING TO THE MOST HIGH

Read Genesis 3:8-13. What are some of the ways that God uses to call us to come out of hiding?

EXPERIENCING HIS POWER AND PRESENCE

In what ways do you tend to hide from God?

Search your heart and pray about how you respond when God calls, "Where are you?"

The one wise thing to do is to draw near to God in penitential prayer, to seek and find reconciliation to Him by faith in the Divine Saviour, that there may be no need and no desire to hide from His face, to shun His voice, to fear the touch of His hand.[1]

— *E. R. Conder and W. Clarkson*

Dear Lord, thank You for caring about where I am. Whether I am hiding or sitting at Your feet, You continually seek my presence. I love You for not letting me stay in the trees. As painful as Your call may be, may I always answer, "Here I am, Lord." *Amen.*

I STAND AT THE DOOR AND KNOCK

*Behold, I stand at the door and knock. If anyone hears
My voice and opens the door, I will come in to him and
dine with him, and he with Me.*

— REVELATION 3:20, NKJV

The church I attended as a young girl had a popular picture hanging in the foyer. This familiar painting portrays Christ dressed in a long white robe, standing outside a quaint cottage. His head is tilted and His hand is just about to knock on the wooden door. I remember someone pointing out to me that there was no doorknob on the outside of the house. The artist had beautifully illustrated this passage in Revelation by showing Christ waiting for someone to hear His call and open the door from the inside.

The context of this verse is Jesus' stern address to the wealthy Laodicean church, which had lapsed into complacency and self-satisfaction. Jesus strongly rebuked them for being lukewarm. In fact, they were so spiritually impoverished that they had grown blind to their own needs. As the Lord called them to repentance, He assured them of His love while He chastened them, encouraging them to be zealous and repent.

Then came His declaration: "Look at me. I stand at the door. I knock. If you hear me call and open the door, I'll come right in and sit down to supper with you" (Revelation 3:20, MSG). How remarkable that our Lord, who was so grieved by His followers' prideful contentment with the world, would even want to be a part of their lives. Yet there He is, standing at the door of their church and at the door of their hearts.

This Scripture is just as relevant today as it was then. Jesus stands at the door of our hearts, just as He did with the Laodiceans. He waits to gain entrance in order to have fellowship with us. He desires our presence. To the disciples, Jesus said, "If anyone loves Me, he will keep My word; and My Father will love him, and We will come to him and make Our home with him" (John 14:23, NKJV). God's desire is for His presence to dwell within us, for Him to be at home in our hearts. Jesus died so that this close, intimate fellowship could be possible.

How paradoxical that Jesus, who is the Door by whom all enter into life with the Most High, must knock on the door of our souls. His posture of standing and waiting exemplifies His patience and graciousness. David said of the Lord, "But You, O Lord, are a God full of compassion, and gracious, longsuffering and abundant in mercy and truth" (Psalm 86:15, NKJV).

Christ's knocking also shows His humility. It is overwhelming to realize that the Lord would humble Himself to stand at the door of human hearts, waiting for lukewarm, busy, self-absorbed people to answer.

Years ago, when my husband and I were calling on people door-to-door to share Christ with them, we carried a sheet of paper outlining the procedure to follow. I loved the first item on the list: "go to the door and knock." If we didn't knock, there would be no reason for anyone to answer. Christ's knock signifies His desire for admittance and demonstrates His great love for us.

Christ indicates that while He stands outside, it is possible for us to hear His voice. It was the custom of the day to call aloud while knocking. When the Lord calls, we know who is knocking outside. He always identifies Himself, though He knocks and calls to us in various ways: His Word, His Spirit, through trials, through others who teach His Word. But Christ has given the homeowner the option of not opening the door; we have the freedom not to answer.

But if we do hear Him and open the door, what blessings He bestows! He comes in to commune with us. This astounding scenario is staggering: the God of the universe knocking on the door of our hearts so that He can enjoy our company. I am always delighted when someone wants to share a meal with me. It means that they want to spend some extended, leisurely time in my company, for a meal is not meant to be consumed hurriedly. Christ's knock is not for a brief greeting at the door — it is for a continuing encounter of intimate sharing, in which He can impart His love, His grace, Himself.

Christ was speaking to the church when He declared that He stands at the door. Whether this verse applies to those outside the church is open for debate — but in this context, the hearers are church members who needed to repent. Christ was waiting to receive them when they opened the door. The Lord knocking on the door of our hearts is like God calling to Adam in the Garden. Both encounters depict the heart of God calling for His own to abide with Him in the shadow of the Almighty. The Most High calls to us and waits for us to respond. He desires to quench our deepest thirst, to satisfy our deepest hunger, and to fill us with His power and presence as we dwell in the secret place of the Most High.

LISTENING TO THE MOST HIGH

Read Revelation 3:20. How do you think the Laodiceans' lives would change if they responded by opening their hearts to Christ?

EXPERIENCING HIS POWER AND PRESENCE

What are the doors in your life that need to be opened to more of Christ's presence and power?

Spend time with the Lord in prayer, responding from your heart to His gracious invitation in Revelation 3:20.

Lord, teach me to listen. The times are noisy and my ears are weary with the thousand raucous sounds which continuously assault them. . . . Let me hear Thee speaking in my heart. Let me get used to the sound of Thy voice, that its tones may be familiar when the sounds of earth die away and the only sound will be the music of Thy speaking voice. Amen.[1]

— A. W. Tozer

Dear Lord, I thirst for a deeper experience of Your presence and power. Thank You for graciously inviting me to dwell with You in the secret place of the Most High. *Amen.*

DON'T BE AFRAID, FOR I AM WITH YOU

*Don't be afraid, for I am with you. Don't be discouraged,
for I am your God. I will strengthen you and help you. I
will hold you up with my victorious right hand.*

— ISAIAH 41:10, NLT

Someone once asked me, "What is your greatest fear?" As I pondered my reply, I remembered this powerful verse in Isaiah 41:10 (NASB), in which God says so clearly, "Do not fear, for I am with you." I memorized this promise from God many years ago, and its truth continually speaks to my heart. Certainly I am not totally fearless, for I am concerned about the possibility of those I love having to endure suffering, and I am a little fearful of how I might die. When I fly or drive on the highway, I'm aware of the accidents that can occur. This is not a perfect world — and that's why God so lovingly speaks to our hearts, "Don't be afraid, for I am with you."

These words of the Lord were originally spoken to comfort and assure Israel before the fearful prospect of their coming captivity. God was not going to abandon His children. The preceding verses had warned that God was sending Cyrus, king of Persia, to execute judgment. The pagan nations would turn to their idols in fear, but God would hand them over as a ransom for Israel. Isaiah 43:3-4 elaborates, "For I am the LORD your God, the Holy One of Israel, your Savior; I have given Egypt as your ransom, [Ethiopia] and Seba in your place. Since you are precious in My sight, since you are honored and I love you" (NASB). Because Israel was precious and loved, God would rescue them. They did not need to live in fear. God used three different names for Himself in this passage, each emphasizing a different facet of His character. "The LORD your God," "the Holy One of Israel," and "your Savior" reinforce His power and preeminence (superiority), His absolute righteousness, and His faithfulness to keep His covenant. These were not the claims of a pagan god; these were the perfect characteristics of the God who loved His people and would never desert them.

Although these verses were written specifically to Israel, they also apply to us as His adopted children. His character remains the same and so does His covenant commitment to all His children. This same almighty, holy, and victorious God proclaims His presence, commitment, strength, and help so that none of His children will be dismayed. When He says, "Fear not, I am with you," He is also speaking to *you*.

The basis for our freedom from fear is the assurance that God is with us. Reverend John McNeill, a Scottish minister, tells the story of when he was a young boy, walking through a lonely glen late at night. Just as he was about to enter the darkest part of his walk, out of the black night he heard the strong, cheery voice of his father calling his name. He relates, "It was my father — the bravest, strongest man I ever knew. Many a time since, when things have been getting very black and gloomy about me, I have heard a voice greater than any earthly parent cry: 'Fear not, for I am with thee.' And lo! *God's foot is rising and falling on the road before us as we tread the journey of life.*"[1]

As the Egyptian army bore down on the Israelites, Moses cried out, "Do not fear!" The exhortation "Do not fear" was given to Joshua as he prepared to lead Israel into Canaan. It was given to Daniel by the angel of the Lord who appeared to explain his visions. Gabriel declared to Mary and Joseph, "Do not fear." Elisha assured Gehazi concerning the army surrounding them, "Do not fear, for those who are with us are more than those who are with them" (2 Kings 6:16, NKJV). To the amazed disciples watching Him walk on water, Jesus said, "Do not fear." Angels met the women at the empty tomb with the comforting words, "Do not fear." In the midst of a violent storm at sea, Paul was reassured with "Do not fear." Throughout history, in any circumstance, God's word to His people has been, "Do not fear!"

God's assurance through the prophet Isaiah is underscored in 41:10 with the reinforcing statement, "Don't be discouraged, for I am your God" (NLT). The word *dismay* means a loss of courage or resolution through the pressure of sudden fear or anxiety. To be dismayed is to be perplexed about how to deal with a situation. Synonyms include *disheartened, scared, dejected, intimidated.* When Elijah was intimidated by Jezebel's threats to kill him, he ran into the wilderness and prayed to die. After an angel ministered to his physical needs, he traveled for forty days and nights to Mount Sinai, where he slept in a cave — anxious, disheartened, and scared. Despite his zealous service to the Lord, it appeared that no one else stood with him. He was perplexed; nothing made sense. Elijah was greatly dismayed.

God met Elijah in the cave and asked, "What are you doing here, Elijah?" The prophet explained how he was the only one left who had not worshiped Baal. Everyone else had forsaken God's covenant, torn down His altars, and killed His prophets. Now Jezebel was seeking Elijah's life. Elijah was desperately in need of being "strengthened" and "upheld."

God's next response was to allow Elijah to witness a fierce wind, a sudden earthquake, and a fire — none of which revealed God's presence. Only a gentle whisper — a still, small voice — revealed to Elijah that God was with him. After all the stressful and exhausting circumstances the prophet had been through, he needed to be reminded that he would draw strength from quietness and confidence, and he needed to know that he was not the only faithful man left, because God had protected a remnant of seven thousand in Israel who had not bowed down to Baal.

I think the Lord was saying, "See, Elijah? You don't need to be dismayed, because I am your God. This means you are not responsible for the world — I am! I know who has been rebellious and who has been faithful. You are not alone! I am with you, and I have made sure there are others united with you in faithfulness to Me."

God strengthened Elijah physically and spiritually by His presence and concern for him. He upheld Elijah by affirming his ministry, extending it through Elisha, and giving him hope for the future. Elijah learned firsthand what Paul would later proclaim: "If God is for us, who can be against us?" (Romans 8:31, NKJV).

I believe that the Lord really does intend that we should live without fear. Therefore, my answer to the question "What is your greatest fear?" is that I don't have a consuming fear that preoccupies my thoughts. I know that in loving concern for my spiritual well-being, God asks me not to fear by trusting Him to strengthen, help, and uphold me in any circumstance. David's testimony in Psalm 27:5 is a comfort: "For in the time of trouble He shall hide me in His pavilion; in the secret place of His tabernacle" (NKJV).

As you dwell in His presence, God also speaks personally to you: "Don't be afraid, for I am with *you* — I am the Lord *your* God, the Holy One of Israel, *your* Savior. Don't be disheartened and discouraged. I will strengthen *you*, help *you*, and uphold *you*."

LISTENING TO THE MOST HIGH
Read Isaiah 41:10. How does the knowledge of God's presence encourage you to release your fears?

EXPERIENCING HIS POWER AND PRESENCE
In which areas of your life are you most afraid that God will not strengthen or help you?

In prayer, ask the Lord to direct these words from Isaiah to your heart, to take hold at a level deeper than all your fears.

Fear nothing but sin.[2]

— *George Herbert*

Father, I am forever grateful that you want to deliver me from fear and that you desire to strengthen, help, and uphold me with your victorious right hand. *Amen.*

BLESSED ARE THOSE WHO TRUST IN THE LORD

But blessed are those who trust in the LORD and have made the LORD their hope and confidence.

— JEREMIAH 17:7, NLT

A popular evening game show features test-your-knowledge kinds of questions, each one accompanied by a multiple-choice set of four possible answers. When contestants are unsure of the correct answer, they may choose from three avenues of help. One option is polling the audience, who is equipped with devices at each seat for voting on their individual answers. Their collective responses are tabulated instantly, and a chart displays the results.

Most contestants choose the answer selected by a majority of the audience. One night, 63 percent of the audience voted for a particular answer, but the contestant was silent as he considered whether to accept their choice or select a different one. I kept thinking, *Go with the audience!* He finally decided on an answer counter to the popular opinion in the studio — and his choice happened to be the right one. Now he knew that he couldn't totally depend on other people. With the next question, he again relied on his own judgment — and discovered that he couldn't really depend on himself, because this time he chose the wrong answer.

"Blessed are those who trust in the LORD" — this statement was made by God Himself, for the prophet Jeremiah prefaced these words with "This is what the LORD says" (Jeremiah 17:5, NLT). But God also declares that those who trust in "mere humans" and turn their hearts away from Him are cursed (17:5, NLT). It is not wrong to trust others, but it becomes wrong when our trust in other people takes precedence over our confidence in the Lord.

When the Israelites were poised to go into Canaan under Joshua's leadership, they depended on the counsel of ten spies concerning the advisability of entering this new land. They trusted in the majority opinion of the spies, and it was wrong. Israel had trusted man's word over God's.

In Jeremiah 17:6, it is intriguing that the Lord compared the person who trusts in people to a shrub in the desert, living in a barren wilderness with no hope for the future. What a perfect picture of the Israelites wandering in the wilderness for forty years! They were exiled to the wilderness until the generation of those who had trusted in man had died. Jeremiah's prophetic words from the Lord were addressed to the Israelite kingdom of Judah, who trusted in false gods and foreign alliances for its welfare. Judah would soon be exiled to Babylon, where the people would understand what it was like to be a shrub in a barren wilderness.

Through His prophet, God addressed two groups of people:

those who trust in man and those who trust in Him. Essentially, these are our choices in life — to walk by faith, trusting God; or to walk by sight, trusting people. Walking by sight means depending wholly upon people for guidance and fulfillment — family, friends, or self. It means trusting only what we can see and touch. As cherished and loving as families can be, however, unfortunately they can also be unloving and hurtful. Joseph experienced slavery and prison as a result of his brothers' hatred and envy. He certainly could not trust his family to love and help him. Even Jesus did not have the full approval of His family during His ministry.

Friends can be supportive and encouraging, but they, too, can disappoint us. Job discovered this reality when his so-called friends aggravated his pain and suffering instead of comforting him. Paul faced this disillusionment as well, as he wrote to Timothy: "The first time I was brought before the judge, no one came with me. Everyone abandoned me" (2 Timothy 4:16, NLT). Here was the dear apostle who had poured out his life for the church, with no one to stand by him when he needed support.

If we choose to walk by sight only to find that family and friends fail us, our only alternative is to go it alone — to become independent of others. We inherit this bent for autonomy from Adam and Eve, who chose to trust themselves instead of God. Sarah, impatient with God's timing in providing a child, encouraged Abraham to conceive a child with her maid, Hagar. How easy it is for us to think we know what is best. Unfortunately, even when we are most confident in ourselves, we are not dependable! Before Jesus was arrested, He told the disciples they would all desert Him. Peter protested, "Even if everyone else deserts you, I will never desert you" (Matthew 26:33, NLT). When Jesus told Peter that in fact he *would* deny Him, Peter insisted, "Even if I have to die with you, I will never deny you!" (verse 35, NLT). Peter's confidence was sincere, but even he could not guarantee his own behavior.

Proverbs 3:5-6 reminds us, "Trust in the LORD with all your heart; do not depend on your own understanding. Seek his will in all you do, and he will show you which path to take" (NLT). This is what God wants us to do. He declares, *"Blessed* are those who trust in Me!" He wants us to spend our lives not like dried-up shrubs in the middle of a wasteland but like trees planted along a riverbank. "Such trees are not bothered by the heat or worried by long months of drought. Their leaves stay green, and they never stop producing fruit" (Jeremiah 17:8, NLT). Our seeking of God's way in our lives enables us to grow, to become strong and productive. We are planted where it is best for us to live, and He uses everything in our lives to work for our good.

It does not always seem that events in our lives work for our good. I found this commentator's explanation helpful in understanding what it means to be blessed by placing our confidence in God: "Trust in God does not prevent the approach of trouble, but it fortifies us against suffering real harm from it."[1]

When Joseph was carried off to Egypt as a slave, Scripture relates that "the LORD was with Joseph" (Genesis 39:2, NKJV). Paul, deserted by his friends, affirmed to Timothy, "But the Lord stood with me and strengthened me" (2 Timothy 4:17, NKJV). Job had the gratification of hearing God say to his friends, "My wrath is aroused against you" (Job 42:7, NKJV).

It does not matter if you have failed to trust God in the past. The blessings of turning your heart back toward Him and walking by faith are yours as soon as you place your hope and confidence in Him. Sarah did have her baby, and her name is mentioned in Hebrews 11 as an example of one who trusted God. Peter was restored by the Lord and became God's chosen leader of the early church. God is eternally trustworthy and as you dwell in His presence, you will always be guided to choose what is right.

LISTENING TO THE MOST HIGH

Read Jeremiah 17:7. How would you describe the blessings of trusting in the Lord?

EXPERIENCING HIS POWER AND PRESENCE

Describe an event or season in your life when you learned the crucial importance of trusting in God rather than in yourself or other people.

In prayer, confess to God your difficulties in trusting Him and ask Him to deepen your hope and confidence in Him.

God has given to us the dangerous privilege of a larger lib-
erty, and the serious responsibility of voluntarily choosing
or rejecting His guidance. But then He vouchsafes this great
help on the simplest of all conditions. We have not to deserve
it, to attain to it by any skill or labour, but simply to trust
with the most childlike faith.[2]

— *W. F. Adeney*

Dear Father, thank You for blessings that trust bestows.
May I always place my hope and confidence in You and You
alone. *Amen.*

I KNOW THE PLANS I HAVE FOR YOU

*"For I know the plans I have for you," says the L*ORD*.*
"They are plans for good and not for disaster,
to give you a future and a hope.

— JEREMIAH 29:11, NLT

"I have only your good in mind. My decisions are made for your welfare. I know what is best for you." Most children have heard these words at one time or another from their parents — usually when one of their requests is being denied. While they're nursing their disappointment, their parents try to convince them that they really do know what is right for them — they really are on their children's side.

God was speaking, in the same manner, to His children who were in exile in Babylon. Certainly, the Israelites were sighing and questioning God's goodness to them. The Exile, which was to last seventy years, was the result of Israel's idolatry. Prompted by God, Jeremiah wrote a letter to the elders, the priests, the prophets, and all the people carried away by Nebuchadnezzar. In it God affirmed that even though His children were being disciplined, His plans were for their welfare and future restoration. Because exile did not necessarily mean imprisonment or enslavement, they were told to build houses, to marry, and to pray for peace while dwelling there.

This period of time in Babylon was to be a displacement, not an abandonment, of daily living. After seventy years, God would perform His good plan for them and return them to Jerusalem. He comforted His children by saying, "For I know the thoughts that I think toward you . . . thoughts of peace and not of evil, to give you a future and a hope" (Jeremiah 29:11, NKJV).

It is a commentary on our misunderstanding of God's love and care that He must repeatedly reassure us of His desire for our well-being. It all began in the Garden of Eden. God, concerned for the welfare of Adam and Eve, commanded them not to eat the fruit of the Tree of the Knowledge of Good and Evil. Unfortunately, Adam and Eve were persuaded that God was keeping something special from them — that His plan was to deny them good things. The Israelites chose not to enter Canaan because they felt that God was sending them into a dangerous country populated with giants. Surely His plans were not for their welfare. Jesus' parable of the prodigal son also illuminates our misunderstanding of God's loving concern for our welfare. The elder brother angrily refused to attend the celebration for his repentant brother's return. He told his father that it was not fair to favor this wayward brother, for he was the faithful son who had never been so honored. Surely his father's good thoughts were not toward him.

Did God have Adam's and Eve's best interests in mind when He told them not to eat the fruit? Yes, because the prohibition was for their protection and welfare. Was it a good plan for the Israelites to enter Canaan? Yes, for God had removed the protection of the Canaanites and they would be easily conquered. Did the elder son have grounds for feeling that his father did not care for him? No, for his father lovingly replied, "Look, dear son, you have always stayed by me, and everything I have is yours" (Luke 15:31, NLT). Wasn't being close to his father and sharing daily with him a sufficient demonstration of his father's love?

God's plans for us are always for our best. Israel's exile helped them realize that living in Jerusalem and worshiping their God was the right and good way to live. After the Exile, God would restore them and they would then call on Him, pray to Him, and seek Him. God promised that He would be found by them and that He would gather them from all the nations. They had a future and a hope: to be reunited with their God.

I was scheduled to speak at two consecutive seminars at a Christian conference center. The first was to be held over the weekend, with the following one at midweek. Halfway through the weekend I lost my voice. I was able to whisper my way through until Sunday. Since I was scheduled to speak again on Tuesday, my doctor prescribed medicine and put me on twenty-four-hour voice rest. On Monday, my voice was no better. The doctor strongly recommended that I not speak for three more days. With a heavy heart, I left the conference center. The director was very kind and asked me to come again another time and speak for the midweek seminar.

Two years later, I traveled back to the conference center after speaking at a couple of churches immediately beforehand. By the time I arrived at the conference center, I was beginning to lose my voice! I was heartbroken and embarrassed. When the director heard my voice, she immediately escorted me to my room so I could be quiet, and she brought lozenges and hot tea with honey.

While I was alone in my room, the Lord spoke these words to my heart: *Cynthia, do you love Me?*

"Yes, Lord, I love You."

Then give Me your voice.

"Oh, Lord, I can't give You my voice! I *have* to speak. I left this conference once before — I can't leave again!"

Cynthia, do you love Me?

"Yes, Lord."

Then give Me your voice.

This did not sound like a good plan to me. How was this good for my welfare? How could my failure to speak further His kingdom? Was I to be in "exile" again? But in the face of His question concerning my love for Him, what could I say but, "Here, Lord, I give You my voice"?

This event was a precious time of trust and surrender. It led me into believing that His thoughts toward me were for peace and not for disaster, even though I didn't understand His purpose. I was able to speak at the conference with a scratchy voice, but the plan for good that God had for me was the same He had for the Israelite exiles — a closer, more intimate relationship with Him. I called upon Him, and He listened. I sought Him in deeper ways, and He was easily found. His plan is always for His children to have a more dependent, wholehearted relationship with Him. Our future and our hope are in His plan for us — and ultimately, to be with Him for eternity.

A few years ago, the parents of some of our close friends stayed in our home while we were away. A few days after our return, a large package was delivered to our door. When we opened the box and removed all the packing material, we discovered a lovely framed, stained-glass rendering of Jeremiah 29:11. As the sun shines through the beautiful colored flowers surrounding the verse, we are continually reminded of the good plans God has for us — plans sovereignly ordained to keep our focus on our eternal future of dwelling with Him in the secret place of the Most High.

LISTENING TO THE MOST HIGH
Meditate on Jeremiah 29:11. How can a consistent dwelling in His presence help you in understanding God's ways and plans?

EXPERIENCING HIS POWER AND PRESENCE
How would you describe God's plans to give you a future and a hope?

As you pray, bring before God any of your concerns about difficult circumstances and ask Him to give you insight and peace about His plans.

The freedom of God consists in the fact that no cause other than Himself produces His acts and no external obstacle impedes them — that His own goodness is the root from which they all grow and His own omnipotence the air in which they all flower.[1]

— *C. S. Lewis*

Dear Father, Your will and Your way are my good and my hope. Thank You. *Amen.*

MY PEACE I GIVE TO YOU

I am leaving you with a gift — peace of mind and heart.
And the peace I give is a gift the world cannot give. So
don't be troubled or afraid.

— JOHN 14:27, NLT

"Visualize world peace" is a slogan that shows up on a lot of bumper stickers these days. "World peace" tends to be the standard answer to the question "If you could have any wish granted, what would it be?" Most people define *peace* as an end to all war and freedom from oppression and crime. By the world's standards, *peace* means outward security, calm, and harmony.

However, the only peace that humans can implement involves external controls. Rarely does anyone say, "I wish people would have peaceful hearts." Perhaps this is because no one can imagine accomplishing such a feat. But there is One, and only One, who can fulfill the desire for inner peace — the Lord Jesus Christ.

During His last hours with His disciples, Jesus lovingly gave them an invaluable gift — peace of mind and heart. His death was imminent, and He consoled them by declaring that His peace was unique to the world. They would need His special peace because He was leaving them, and the coming events would be confusing and turbulent. He did not want them to be troubled or afraid, so He gave them a peace that would provide internal comfort and rest, regardless of what happened to them externally.

Jesus is the only One who can do this because He is the "Prince of Peace" (Isaiah 9:6, NKJV). Through His death on the cross, He purchased our peace with God. Paul declared, "Therefore, since we have been made right in God's sight by faith, we have peace with God because of what Jesus Christ our Lord has done for us" (Romans 5:1, NLT). Jesus said, "*My* peace I give to you" — and peace is only His to give. His peace cannot be earned or bought; it is a gift of grace, received by faith when we accept Christ as our Savior and Lord. The first peace we experience is the outcome of being reconciled to God.

The peace we experience from Christ is different from the peace the world offers. One scholar writes,

> The world gives to the body; Christ to the soul. The world gives to the outward and transient in man; Christ to the inward and eternal. The world only supplies music for the physical ear, and sceneries for the physical eye; Christ supplies music for the soul, and spiritual sceneries of unspeakable beauty to the eye of faith. The world supplies the lowest part of man — his passions and animal propensities; but Christ furnishes the highest part of him — his reason, faith, conscience — and satisfies his immortal aspirations and wants.[1]

Worldly peace must be sought after, purchased, and renewed. Getting away for a period of time, meditating on anything that promises peace, communing with nature, acquiring possessions, seeking status, withdrawing from people — all are forms of the human search for peace from the world. It can be a consuming task for an elusive goal, and worldly peace is fleeting because it depends on circumstances, and ultimately we cannot control circumstances. Certainly the apostle Paul could not expect peace from his unpredictable and strenuous life. To the Corinthians he testified, "We are hard-pressed on every side, yet not crushed; we are perplexed, but not in despair; persecuted, but not forsaken; struck down, but not destroyed. . . . Even though our outward man is perishing, yet the inward man is being renewed day by day" (2 Corinthians 4:8-9,16, NKJV). To the Colossians he wrote, "And let the peace of God rule in your hearts" (Colossians 3:15, NKJV). Only the peace he received from Christ enabled him to say that he was not crushed, in despair, struck down, or destroyed.

This inner peace guards us while we live in a difficult world. There are two essential ways of maintaining peaceful hearts and minds. The first is to pray about everything. J. B. Phillips translates Philippians 4:6-7, "Don't worry over anything whatever; tell God every detail of your needs in earnest and thankful prayer, and the peace of God, which transcends human understanding, will keep constant guard over your hearts and minds as they rest in Christ Jesus."

I can testify to the wonderful truth of these verses, but it seems that I must continually learn to include thankfulness in my prayers. Recently, I was deeply burdened, and I was certainly telling God every detail of my concern, but I continued to carry the weight of my situation. It wasn't until I began to express thankfulness that I experienced the peace that keeps constant guard over my heart and mind. It was a struggle, but this was my prayer: "Lord, I don't like these circumstances. I wish they would just go away. I don't want to deal with having to work through these hard times. But, Lord, I'm thankful that You know all about this. I thank You that You are leading and guiding me. I thank You that Your grace is sufficient. I thank You that this is not really my life, but Yours, and You are free to mold me and conform me according to Your good pleasure." It wasn't until I prayed this from my heart that His peace invaded my soul, and I was able to move through the circumstances resting in Christ Jesus.

The second way to continue in God's peace is to abide in Christ and trust His ways. A beautiful verse I memorized years ago is Isaiah 26:3, "You will keep him in perfect peace, whose mind is stayed on You, because he trusts in You" (NKJV). "Staying" our mind involves fixing our eyes on Jesus, meditating on the truth of His Word, spending time with the Lord. Trusting that God's plans are for our welfare can relieve a lot of anxiety and replace it with peace.

There is much evidence throughout the New Testament that the disciples did indeed receive the Lord's peace. I've always been impressed with the peace that protected Peter when he was in prison. Herod had just executed James, which pleased the Jews. The king then arrested Peter; apparently he was next on the list to be killed. I love the Scripture that describes Peter's heart and mind while awaiting trial:

> And when Herod was about to bring him out, that night
> Peter was sleeping, bound with two chains between two
> soldiers; and the guards before the door were keeping the
> prison. Now behold, an angel of the Lord stood by him, and
> a light shone in the prison; and he struck Peter on the side
> and raised him up, saying, "Arise quickly!" (Acts 12:6-7,
> NKJV)

What amazes me is that the angel had to *strike* Peter to wake him up! On the night before he might die, Peter slept soundly. He had received the gracious gift of Christ's peace, and he was not anxious or fearful.

The Lord lovingly speaks to your heart also, "I am leaving you with a gift — peace of mind and heart. And the peace I give is a gift the world cannot give. So don't be troubled or afraid" (John 14:27, NLT). Will you accept His gift? It is found in abundance as we dwell in His presence.

LISTENING TO THE MOST HIGH

Read John 14:27. How would you describe the difference between the peace that the world gives and the peace that Jesus gives?

EXPERIENCING HIS POWER AND PRESENCE

Describe a time when you were especially aware of the peace of Christ guarding your heart and mind.

Choose an anxiety or fear that has been troubling you and bring it to God in prayer, either alone or with a friend.

The world can neither give nor take, Nor can they compre-hend, The peace of God which Christ has brought — the peace which knows no end.[2]

—*J. R. Thomson*

Dear Lord, thank You for Your peace that stands guard over my heart and mind, keeping away anxiety and fear. *Amen.*

I HAVE OVERCOME THE WORLD

These things I have spoken to you, that in Me you may have peace. In the world you will have tribulation; but be of good cheer, I have overcome the world.

— JOHN 16:33, NKJV

For fourteen years, two friends and I decided to meet for mutual accountability and prayer. We met weekly for the first few years, and we formed a threefold cord that could not easily be broken. We would usually eat lunch, share what was going on in our lives, and then spend time in prayer. Over a period of time, one friend developed breast cancer. We prayed her through surgery and chemotherapy. Now, several years later, she is cancer free. Two years ago, my other dear friend began to exhibit flu-like symptoms for several weeks. The doctor prescribed what he felt she needed, but she continued to get weaker. She could not maintain her balance and was admitted to the hospital for tests. It turned out that she had a very rare disease, and it progressively took her life. It was just as Jesus said — in the world we experience painful tribulation.

On the night of Christ's betrayal before going into the garden to pray, He left His disciples with this powerful "benediction": "I've told you all this so that trusting me, you will be unshakable and assured, deeply at peace. In this godless world you will continue to experience difficulties. But take heart! I've conquered the world" (John 16:33, MSG).

Jesus Himself was unshakably committed to His Father's will, even though He faced the agony of the Cross and the impending desertion of His disciples. He was at peace because the Father was with Him. It is this same abiding peace that He imparted to His followers: "This is spiritual peace. We are not supposed to think that Christians are exempt from the cares and the calamities of life, that outward circumstances and human society are all to combine in order to his preservation from the troubles which are incidental to human life. But there may be calm within even while the storm rages without. The heart may be set free from fear."

Jesus prepared His disciples for tribulation by telling them that the world would hate them. "If the world hates you, remember that it hated me first. The world would love you as one of its own if you belonged to it, but you are no longer part of the world. I chose you to come out of the world, so it hates you" (John 15:18-19, NLT). Tribulation is affliction, difficulty, suffering, distress. The Lord wants all His disciples to know that while we are here on earth, we will experience hard times. Someone wrote me a note at a conference with this insightful comment, "For some reason, Christians think they should get a discount on suffering!" Paul strengthened the church by writing, "We must through many tribulations enter the kingdom of God" (Acts 14:22, NKJV), and "all who desire to live godly in

Christ Jesus will suffer persecution" (2 Timothy 3:12, NKJV).

Since tribulation is such an integral part of this life, Jesus gives us His peace and the lasting encouragement that He has overcome the world. It cannot defeat us, for Jesus, through His death on the cross, has conquered it and His victory is ours. The world's hate need no longer intimidate us or harm us spiritually. It can try to conquer us through outright persecution or through its subtle enticements; either way we are to be of good cheer. One commentator explains, "Take heart! means 'Be courageous.' (In the New Testament the word *tharseo* [take heart, be courageous, cheer up] was spoken only by the Lord.)"[1]

The way that we cheerfully overcome the world is through our trust in Christ. The apostle John wrote, "For whatever is born of God overcomes the world. And this is the victory that has overcome the world — our faith" (1 John 5:4, NKJV). Our faith in Christ enables us to overcome evil in whatever form it may present itself to us. It means believing that we can do all things through Christ who strengthens us. Shadrach, Meshach, and Abednego overcame the world by trusting God when they were thrown into the furnace. Joseph overcame the world when he fled from Potiphar's seductive wife. Paul and Silas overcame the world when, after being severely beaten and put in prison, they prayed and sang hymns.

Paul seemed to stand on a mountaintop and shout, "Can anything ever separate us from Christ's love? Does it mean he no longer loves us if we have trouble or calamity, or are persecuted, or hungry, or destitute, or in danger, or threatened with death? . . . No, despite all these things, overwhelming victory is ours through Christ, who loved us" (Romans 8:35,37, NLT). No matter what kind of tribulation we encounter, it can never isolate us from Christ.

My precious friend continually gave testimony to Christ's peace in her heart. Her unswerving faith was evidence that in the midst of suffering it is possible to dwell in the secret place of the Most High. And His peace is ours also as we persevere in tribulation and experience His overcoming power. In the midst of our godless world, filled with difficulties, how needful it is that we dwell in His presence.

LISTENING TO THE MOST HIGH
Read John 16:33. In what sense has Jesus overcome the world?

EXPERIENCING HIS POWER AND PRESENCE
In what ways does Jesus' statement "I have overcome the world" give you encouragement in facing life's inevitable troubles?

In prayer, reflect upon this verse and ask God to fill your heart with a sense of "good cheer."

There is no peace in the world; there is no tribulation in Christ.[2]

— *B. Thomas*

Dear Lord, thank you that I can take heart, be of good cheer and have peace in the midst of a turbulent world. *Amen.*

STORE YOUR TREASURES IN HEAVEN

Don't store up treasures here on earth, where moths eat them and rust destroys them, and where thieves break in and steal. Store your treasures in heaven, where moths and rust cannot destroy, and thieves do not break in and steal. Wherever your treasure is, there the desires of your heart will also be.

— MATTHEW 6:19-21, NLT

When our son-in-law received his orders from the U.S. Air Force to move to Korea for two years, my daughter had to begin the arduous process of storing their furniture and most of their possessions. Several beautiful antiques inherited from relatives went into storage. When they returned to the States, their furniture was shipped and delivered. As they unpacked the boxes, they became progressively more heartsick. The oak dining hutch and table were severely warped, the lovely Queen Anne sofa was water-damaged, the pink and white threads on the French petit-point chairs were frayed, the leg of the wing-back chair was broken. Just about everything they had stored was damaged in some way. They were surrounded with books, linens, and clothes that smelled and a houseful of broken and ruined furniture. Our children's storage of their "treasures" was a necessity, but it bore painful testimony to the potential ravages of storing possessions.

Knowing our nature, Jesus addressed our desire to accumulate things. The Lord did not say it is wrong to have possessions. He said that our investment in spiritual treasure should take precedence over our investment in material treasure. We are not to be consumed with accumulating and storing things at the expense of our spiritual life. He wants us to understand that material things are temporary; they can be destroyed or stolen.

In ancient Oriental cultures, beautiful clothing was prized as ornamentation and an indication of wealth. Perhaps this is why Samson offered thirty linen garments and thirty changes of clothes for anyone who could answer his riddle (Judges 14:12). This desire to acquire clothes prompted Jesus to point out that our treasure can be destroyed by a lowly moth. I often think of the few dresses my grandmother owned. She never had to stand in front of her closet debating what to wear, nor did she ever worry about moths eating any stored-away clothes. Rust destroys gold and silver, and wealth certainly attracts thieves. Earthly riches can consume us by causing us to worry about them, care for them, protect them. Jesus simply instructs us not to spend our lives storing up treasures that are short-lived and subject to theft.

In response to a man's request that Jesus tell his brother to divide the inheritance with him, Jesus says, "Beware! Guard against every kind of greed. Life is not measured by how much you own" (Luke 12:15,

NLT). He then proceeds to tell the parable of the rich fool who began to accumulate an abundance of crops and goods. This man, instead of desiring to be a good steward of his wealth, decided to tear down his barns and build larger and greater storage for his bounty. Then, after spending time and money for increased storage, he died. Jesus concluded with this statement: "Yes, a person is a fool to store up earthly wealth but not have a rich relationship with God" (Luke 12:21, NLT).

Having a rich relationship with God is the ultimate measure of what real life is all about. What occupies our heart determines what we value most. The Lord taught that instead of being absorbed in obtaining the world's goods, we are to store up treasures in heaven. Eternal treasures are safe and secure from moths, rust, thieves, and sudden death.

For those who do have wealth, Paul felt it necessary to give special instructions. He wrote to Timothy, "Command those who are rich in this present age not to be haughty, nor to trust in uncertain riches but in the living God, who gives us richly all things to enjoy. Let them do good, that they be rich in good works, ready to give, willing to share, storing up for themselves a good foundation for the time to come, that they may lay hold on eternal life" (1 Timothy 6:17-19, NKJV).

Paul said that he was given the privilege of preaching the "unsearchable riches of Christ" (Ephesians 3:8, NKJV). Our riches are in Christ Jesus. Our inheritance is life with Christ: "It is by his great mercy that we have been born again, because God raised Jesus Christ from the dead. Now we live with great expectation, and we have a priceless inheritance — an inheritance that is kept in heaven for you, pure and undefiled, beyond the reach of change and decay" (1 Peter 1:3-4, NLT). Storing treasure in heaven involves investing our lives in the truth found in Scripture, loving and trusting God, serving and sharing with others, and seeking first His kingdom and righteousness. Only when our hearts are set on Christ can we begin to store treasure in heaven. "A treasure laid up on earth chains the heart with it to earth," observed commentator P. C. Barker, "for wherever the treasure is the heart is; whatever the treasure is, it is fashioning the heart to it. 'What folly to store your treasure in the place you must soon leave!' What folly to have as treasure that which enslaves but never ennobles!"[1]

I often drive by a lovely church that used to be surrounded by a natural desert landscape. For years this untouched land had somehow escaped becoming a fast-food haven or gas station. So it was with much dismay that I watched the clearing of the cactus and the invasion of concrete trucks. Soon a sign announced that a self-storage complex was being built. I was a little surprised because this was the third such complex near our home. Certainly there are times when a storage unit is a necessity, and it can be quite useful, but the fact that there are so many public storage buildings is a commentary on the American bent to collect and accumulate. Now whenever I drive down Speedway Boulevard and see the church and the storage complex standing side by side, I am reminded of my two choices in how I want to store my treasure — temporal storage that may result in ruin or theft or eternal storage that is secure and can guard the most precious treasure, my heart.

LISTENING TO THE MOST HIGH
Read Matthew 6:19-21. For believers today, what do you think are the earthly "treasures" most likely to compete with an eternal perspective?

EXPERIENCING HIS POWER AND PRESENCE

Take time to access your earthly storage in light of what you are storing for eternity. Are there any practical changes you can make?

Spend some time with the Lord in prayer, asking Him to redirect your heart toward heavenly treasure.

Place your treasure in the only secure cabinet. Store your jewels where you can never lose them. Put them all in Jesus Christ. Set your affection on Him. Place all your hope in His merit. Deposit all your trust in His effectual blood. Put your joy in His presence.[2]

— *Charles H. Spurgeon*

Lord, teach me to be wise in the use of that which is temporary and passionate for that which is eternal. *Amen.*

I AM THE FIRST AND THE LAST

This is what the LORD says — Israel's King and Redeemer,
the LORD of Heaven's Armies: "I am the First and the
Last; there is no other God. Who is like me? Let him step
forward and prove to you his power. Let him do as I have
done since ancient times when I established a people and
explained its future. Do not tremble; do not be afraid.
Did I not proclaim my purposes for you long ago?
You are my witnesses — is there any other God?
No! There is no other Rock — not one!"

— ISAIAH 44:6-8, NLT

Several years ago I was asked to speak at a conference in the Far East. There was a scheduled time for me to interact with those attending by answering their questions. Index cards were provided for the women to write down their questions and during lunch

I read through them. I was somewhat amazed when I read the following concern: "My roommate prays to an idol, and she has gotten everything she has asked for. How can I share the Lord with her?"

Isaiah, God's prophet for more than sixty years, delivered a clear message to the future Israelite exiles in Babylon. God wanted to comfort and warn His children while they were living in a foreign country consumed with idolatry. The weary exiles might begin to lose heart and think that God had forgotten them. They might listen to their captors and start to believe in the superiority of the Babylonians' gods.

So God spoke: "I am the First and the Last; there is no other God." John the apostle wrote of the Lord in this way, "I am the Alpha and the Omega, the First and the Last, the Beginning and the End" (Revelation 22:13, NLT). God alone is God! Moses reminded the Israelites, "Search all of history, from the time God created people on the earth until now. . . . Has any other god dared to take a nation for himself out of another nation by means of trials, miraculous signs, wonders, war, a strong hand, a powerful arm, and terrifying acts? Yet that is what the LORD your God did for you in Egypt, right before your eyes. . . . The LORD is God both in heaven and on earth, and there is no other" (Deuteronomy 4:32,34,39, NLT).

God had proven His care for His children in the past. Did they not remember His purpose for them?

> "But you are my witnesses, O Israel!" says the LORD. "You are my servant. You have been chosen to know me, believe in me, and understand that I alone am God. There is no other God — there never has been, and there never will be. I, yes I, am the LORD, and there is no other Savior. First I predicted your rescue, then I saved you and proclaimed it to the world. No foreign god has ever done this. . . . From

eternity to eternity I am God. No one can snatch anyone out of my hand. No one can undo what I have done." (Isaiah 43:10-13, NLT)

Isaiah continued to remind Israel of the futility of worshiping an idol made by man — an idol who could not see, hear, walk, or know anything. "Who but a fool would make his own god — an idol that cannot help him one bit? All who worship idols will be disgraced" (Isaiah 44:10-11, NLT).

The prophet Jeremiah was confronted with a similar situation. He was prophesying to the remnant of Judah and admonishing them for their worship of idols. But the people responded by saying, "We will not listen to your messages from the LORD! We will do whatever we want. We will burn incense and pour out liquid offerings to the Queen of Heaven just as much as we like. . . . For in those days we had plenty to eat, and we were well off and had no troubles!" (Jeremiah 44:16-17, NLT). Like the young woman's roommate, the people of Judah were more than content to worship an idol because their lives were good; they had everything they wanted. They didn't need the Lord.

As I prayed over the question of witnessing to an idol-worshiping roommate, I was prompted to answer in this way: "Health and pleasant circumstances may seem to coincide with sacrifices to an idol just as the Israelites testified of their worship of the Queen of Heaven. But I would encourage you to ask your friend to make this request of her idol, 'Idol, can you forgive my sins and grant me eternal life?' — for this is the most crucial, life-changing question that truly needs answering."

Because those who spend their lives bowing down to idols are foolish and will one day stand before the Lord in shame, in great compassion God tenderly said, "I am the First and the Last; there is no other God." Do you need these words of love? Is there something or someone other than God who is first in your life? An idol can be a person — someone you may love more than God. An idol can be material — an out-of-balance life continually seeking to accumulate wealth and possessions. An idol can be an inner pattern — the craving for an honored status or position. An idol can be anything that we cling to so passionately that we think we cannot live without it. Some dear saint gave this definition of an idol: anything that, if taken away, would cause you to blame God.

But the Lord, Israel's King and Redeemer, the Lord Almighty, said, "I am the First and the Last; there is no other God. . . . There is no other Rock — not one!" Some idols may be made out of rock, but God is the only Rock, the only One who is strong and stable. The only One who sees, hears, knows, and loves His children. The only One who wants us to dwell in the secret place of the Most High. The only One who can forgive our sins and grant eternal life — for He is the First and the Last.

LISTENING TO THE MOST HIGH

Read Isaiah 44:9-20. What reasons does the Lord give for proclaiming, "I am the First and the Last; there is no other God"?

EXPERIENCING HIS POWER AND PRESENCE

Take time to examine your life to see if there is anyone or anything that you cling to or desire more than the Lord.

Spend some time in prayer proclaiming that God is your rock and He is indeed the first and the last in your life.

Whatever a man seeks, honours, or exalts more than God, this is the god of idolatry.[1]

— *William Ullathorne*

Father, help me to see what I might prize more than my relationship with You. Help me to seek, honor, and exalt You. *Amen.*

BUT ON THIS ONE I WILL LOOK

"For all those things My hand has made, And all those things exist," Says the Lord. *"But on this one will I look: On him who is poor and of a contrite spirit, And who trembles at My word."*

— Isaiah 66:2, nkjv

Have you ever spotted someone you knew in a crowd and tried to get her attention? My husband and I were part of a "moving herd" at a football game. As we slowly made our way up the ramp, I saw a friend across the packed crowd. I knew it was hopeless, but I still called out her name — of course there was no response. As I watched her, she did seem to turn in my direction, so I began to wave frantically and call out to her, but she turned away — oblivious to the fact that someone was trying to get her attention. Because she was not even looking at the crowd for a familiar face, we missed each other.

Not so with our God. He specifically announces whom He is always looking for, whom He will always see: "What I care for are humble, broken creatures, who stand in awe of all I say" (Isaiah 66:2, MOFFATT). My immediate thought is that these dear people are easily found because their presence would be quite obvious in a crowd! It is an astonishing thought that God *looks, beholds, regards* those who revere Him. God takes special notice of His children because they are precious to Him. The chronicler of Scripture observed, "For the eyes of the LORD run to and fro throughout the whole earth, to show Himself strong on behalf of those whose heart is loyal to Him" (2 Chronicles 16:9, NKJV). God searches for and sets His eyes upon His children who love Him and are looking to Him. His purpose is to strengthen those who humbly acknowledge His place in their lives.

Jesus taught that the greatest in the kingdom of God were those who humbled themselves as little children. How does a small child demonstrate humility? Our two-year-old grandson gets up every morning excited about a new day. He is not anxious over whether his needs will be met. He stays close to his parents and, most of the time, listens closely to their instruction and warnings. He is pure. He is not ambitious! He is wonderfully content with where he is and who he is. He never questions his parents' love for him, and he is confident in their care of him. His life is one of simple trust. Can this be what the Lord is looking for? A child who trusts his Father implicitly? A child who is at rest with his place and position in life? A child who simply receives the grace extended to him, secure in his innate confidence that it will never stop?

A. W. Tozer commented,

> The meek man is not a human mouse afflicted with a sense
> of his own inferiority. Rather, he may be in his moral life as

bold as a lion and as strong as Samson; but he has stopped being fooled about himself. He has accepted God's estimate of his own life. He knows he is as weak and helpless as God has declared him to be, but paradoxically, he knows at the same time that he is, in the sight of God, more important than angels. In himself nothing; in God, everything.[1]

It follows that those who are humble will naturally be contrite of spirit. A humble person recognizes that she is destitute without God. She knows that her bent is to sin against the One who unconditionally loves and accepts her. The disciple who was the chosen leader of the Twelve denied knowing the Lord Jesus, not once, but three times. Peter, overwhelmed by his betrayal, went out and wept bitterly. He was repentant, broken, contrite in spirit. Later, the Lord tenderly "looked" to him and restored him. David sinned with Bathsheba and ordered her husband, Uriah, to the front of the battle where he would certainly be killed. When confronted with his sin by Nathan, he said, "I have sinned against the LORD" (2 Samuel 12:13, NKJV). Broken and contrite, he cried, "Restore to me the joy of Your salvation, and uphold me by Your generous Spirit. . . . The sacrifices of God are a broken spirit, a broken and a contrite heart — these, O God, You will not despise" (Psalm 51:12,17, NKJV).

Children are often afraid to confess wrongdoing for fear of the punishment they will receive. It is humbling and amazing that when we repent, God responds in order to restore us, not condemn us. Manasseh, king of Judah, committed such dreadful abominations against God that he was carried away captive to Babylonia. In torment, Manasseh humbled himself greatly before God. The Lord *looked* to Manesseh, heard his prayers, and restored him as king of Judah. God did not despise Manasseh; He was pleased by his contrite spirit.

God is also pleased when we honor His Word for He uses His spoken and written Word to humble and correct His children:

> All Scripture is inspired by God and is useful to teach us what is true and to make us realize what is wrong in our lives. It corrects us when we are wrong and teaches us to do what is right. God uses it to prepare and equip his people to do every good work. (2 Timothy 3:16-17, NLT)

The writer of Hebrews further defines the power of the Scriptures: "For the word of God is alive and powerful. It is sharper than the sharpest two-edged sword, cutting between soul and spirit, between joint and marrow. It exposes our innermost thoughts and desires" (Hebrews 4:12, NLT). No wonder God pays attention to those who tremble at His Word!

Webster defines *tremble* as "to shake involuntarily (as with fear or cold)." Perhaps to tremble at the Word is to approach the Scriptures cautiously and seriously in holy fear, knowing their power. Moffatt translates *tremble* as to "stand in awe." Rotherham's interpretation for *tremble* is "careth anxiously for my Word." The one who trembles before the Scriptures is "a good worker, one who does not need to be ashamed and who correctly explains the word of truth" (2 Timothy 2:15, NLT). She desires to know the Word, to listen to it, and to obey it.

Lot's wife, however, did not tremble at God's Word: "Run for your lives! . . . Don't look back!" (Genesis 19:17, NLT). These words were given for her welfare and protection, yet she was not willing to do what the Lord had said, and she forfeited her life. God's Word is for our instruction and benefit. "Forgive, rejoice, be holy" — these words are meant to pierce our hearts, to teach and guide us. "'Is not My word like a fire?' says the LORD, 'And like a hammer that breaks the rock in pieces?'" (Jeremiah 23:29, NKJV).

Are you humbly dependent upon the Lord, sensitive to sin in your life? Do you, in brokenness, repent before a God who does not condemn you but wants to restore you? Do you honor and hold dear the Word of God, desiring to obey His commands? Then be assured, dear friend, that the almighty God picks you out among the crowd because He is devoted to you. His look is one of tenderness and love. He wants to show Himself mighty on your behalf. You don't even have to wave.

LISTENING TO THE MOST HIGH

Read Isaiah 66:2. How would you describe the differences in attitude and behavior between someone with a "poor and contrite spirit" and a person dominated by arrogance and pride?

EXPERIENCING HIS POWER AND PRESENCE

Take a moment to "look" at your own life in terms of your humble attitude, contrite spirit, and regard for the Word.

Spend some time in prayer asking the Lord to impress upon your heart any need you have to humble yourself, to confess, or to desire His Word.

When all my endeavour is turned toward Thee because all Thy endeavour is turned toward me; when I look unto Thee alone with all my attention, nor ever turn aside the eyes of my mind, because Thou dost enfold me with Thy constant regard; when I direct my love toward Thee alone because Thou, who art Love's self hast turned Thee toward me alone. And what, Lord, is my life, save that embrace wherein Thy delightsome sweetness doth so lovingly enfold me?[2]

— Nicholas Cusa

Dear Father, may I be sensitive to Your Spirit's promptings and may You always look upon me with joy. *Amen.*

YOUR NAMES ARE WRITTEN IN HEAVEN

Nevertheless do not rejoice in this, that the spirits are subject to you, but rather rejoice because your names are written in heaven.

— LUKE 10:20, NKJV

A friend shared with me a precious moment of truth that a couple experienced when they received some devastating news. As his wife wept, the husband gently took her hand and offered this perspective, "Sweetheart, no matter how crushing this situation is, we must remember that the most critical problem we face here on earth has already been resolved." That critical problem was where they would spend eternity: since each of them had a personal relationship with Jesus Christ, their future home was secure. In light of all their difficulties here on earth, it was reassuring to remember that they were God's children and they were not alone in facing this trial. They could look forward to the time when all earthly trials would fade in the light of God's coming glory.

Jesus pointed His disciples toward an eternal perspective when they returned from a successful ministry trip. He had sent out a group of seventy disciples in pairs to visit the surrounding villages and towns to prepare the way for His ministry. He had granted them authority over Satan, and the returning missionaries told Him joyfully about their power over the enemy: "Lord, even the demons obey us when we use your name!" (Luke 10:17, NLT). Jesus shared their elation and observed that He saw the power of Satan broken as quick as lightning at their command. He declared that He had granted them protection not only from Satan, but also from serpents and scorpions (perhaps referring to wicked and crafty men or demonic spirits). But even as Jesus affirmed these triumphant men in their ministry, He pointedly added a *Nevertheless* to His response: awesome as their miracles were, they were to rejoice even more that their names were written in heaven.

The apostle John underscored the importance of our names being written in heaven when he described the judgment of the great white throne. Standing before this throne are the dead, great and small. Books are opened, and they are judged by their works and what is written in the books. One book in particular is mentioned: "And anyone whose name was not found recorded in the Book of Life was thrown into the lake of fire" (Revelation 20:15, NLT). It is no wonder, then, that Jesus encouraged His band of rejoicing missionaries that having their names written in the Book of Life was the first and foremost blessing in which to rejoice.

Jesus' teaching in the Sermon on the Mount may have been echoing in the ears of these disciples. They might have recalled

Jesus saying that not everyone who calls Him "Lord" will enter the kingdom of heaven, only those who obey His Father. He cited the example of those who will say on Judgment Day, "'Lord! Lord! We prophesied in your name and cast out demons in your name and performed many miracles in your name.' But I will reply, 'I never knew you. Get away from me, you who break God's laws'" (Matthew 7:22-23, NLT). Evidently these "unauthorized" disciples were false prophets, whose names were not written in the Book of Life. They were examples of Paul's great passage on love in 1 Corinthians 13; although they prophesied and "moved mountains," their deeds were worthless because they were not done with love.

Recently I was pleased to receive a book from a friend titled *One Hundred Christian Women Who Changed the Twentieth Century.* As I began to read it, I turned to the table of contents and found that there was an entire section devoted to women who had written Bible studies. The idea of my being included among these godly women had not occurred to me when I opened the book, but now as I read the list of Bible study authors, I felt a twinge of disappointment because my name was not there! As I sat in the chair, I heard in my heart these gentle thoughts from the Lord: *Cynthia, even if your name were included in this book, you are not to rejoice about such things. You are to rejoice only and always that your name is written in the Book of Life.*

This truth is also for you. The wellspring of your rejoicing should be in the incredible fact that your belief in Christ as Savior grants you eternal life. The apostle John wrote, "But as many as received Him, to them He gave the right to become children of God, to those who believe in His name" (John 1:12, NKJV). Have you experienced the joy of becoming a child of God by believing in the Lord Jesus Christ? Are you confident that your name is written in heaven? Perhaps you are already a disciple, and like the seventy you are ministering with power in His name. Can you step back and thank the Lord that your greatest joy is not in successful service but in knowing that your name is written in heaven? Or, you may feel that you are *not* doing monumental things for God. Can you look past your spiritual insecurities and still rejoice because your name is written in the Book of Life?

Jesus never wanted His disciples to get caught up in a power trip of what they were accomplishing, for the greatest accomplishment in any life is God's saving grace. To help us keep our eyes on Him, the Lord graciously and lovingly speaks to our hearts, "Rejoice that your names are recorded in heaven" (Luke 10:20, NASB).

LISTENING TO THE MOST HIGH
Read Luke 10:20. Why do you think Jesus chose a moment of triumph in His disciples' lives to give them this teaching?

EXPERIENCING HIS POWER AND PRESENCE
What are the obstacles or distractions that keep you from rejoicing in knowing that your name is written in the Book of Life?

Take some time to praise God as you reflect on His words to you, *Rejoice because your name is written in heaven.* (If you are uncertain about whether these words apply to you, reread John 1:12. Place your belief in Jesus, if you have not already done so. Then ask God to confirm in your heart that you have become His child.)

Saving graces are more to be rejoiced in than spiritual gifts.[1]
— *Matthew Henry*

Dear Lord, I do rejoice in Your gracious salvation. Help me to remember how precious it is and how I need to keep my focus on eternity. *Amen.*

SHUT THE DOOR

But when you pray, go away by yourself, shut the door
behind you, and pray to your Father in private. Then
your Father, who sees everything, will reward you.

— MATTHEW 6:6, NLT

Spending special time in communion with the Lord daily is central to my desire in nurturing my relationship with Him. Quite often I begin to pray with expectations of unhurried, undistracted time to sit in God's presence. But inevitably my mind dredges up urgent requests, inconsequential facts, or mundane tasks that seem to demand immediate attention, and I am drawn away from the communion He offers.

What can we do to overcome distractions that keep us from the intimacy we seek during prayer? When Jesus gave His disciples specific instructions on how to pray, He emphasized getting alone and shutting the door (see Matthew 6:6). One reason for seclusion is to keep from drawing attention to ourselves. Another is to shut the door to the outside world and withdraw for special, focused time with the Lord. When I spend time in a quiet place with the God of the universe, I want to close the door on everything that would disturb or hinder me. As I do this, I make a commitment to slow down and allow myself to experience His presence. I set my heart's attention on the living God, recognizing the high privilege and blessing of intimacy with Him.

In that quiet, intimate space with the Lord, here are a few things that keep me focused on communion with Him.

I often *read Scripture first.* George Mueller, a great man of prayer, wrote that he would often spend up to a half hour suffering from wandering thoughts before he really began to pray. Then he made a simple discovery that helped him eliminate distraction during prayer: He read and meditated on God's Word *first,* then he spent time in prayer. God speaks to us through the Scriptures. When we read His Word before we pray, our hearts are better prepared to respond in prayer to what He has already shown us.

Another way to eliminate distractions in prayer is to *pray out loud or in writing.* The act of speaking forces us to articulate our thoughts, anxieties, and requests more clearly. Praying aloud also causes us to slow down. If our hearts are heavy with the pressures of life, our thought lives may be a flood of anxiety. Speaking our prayers instead of just thinking them allows us to address one issue at a time and can help stem our anxious thoughts by bringing them before the throne of grace one by one.

Writing out our prayers similarly helps keep us focused. As with speaking, writing slows our thoughts and helps us concentrate. Another great benefit of recording our prayers is that we can reread them later. Our written prayers create a unique record of our concerns and God's faithful responses.

I also *pray Scripture.* Often as I read God's Word, I find myself praying several verses back to Him, both for myself or for others. I enjoy praying through many of the psalms. And Paul's prayers for the believers, found in his Epistles, have transformed my prayers. I've copied several of them and use them to guide me as I speak with the Lord about those He has brought to mind. Praying Scripture enables me to pray more for the Lord's eternal perspective than for the temporal and is most helpful in keeping my thoughts stayed on Him.

Giving thanks is another aspect that Scripture encourages me to bring into my time with the Lord: "Devote yourselves to prayer, being watchful and thankful" (Colossians 4:2, NIV). Choosing to give thanks helps me remember God's blessings and faithfulness as I am in His presence, instead of restlessly dwelling on the difficulties of my life. A few years ago I began to ask the Lord to show me His goodness. I realized I often did not acknowledge God's hand in my life. I was oblivious to His loving attention to me, and, as a result, I did not have an attitude of thanksgiving — especially in prayer. Slowly, I have been able to come to the Lord with a more thankful heart. I am now more likely to recognize and give thanks for small blessings, the ones that can be easy to miss or taken for granted: a friend who calls to encourage, a new thought from Scripture, protection while driving, a sense of His presence.

Finally, I greatly enjoy *talking with the Lord while walking.* Something about the active nature of walking helps me concentrate. Most of the time, very few things disturb me while I am on a walk. I feel comfortable with any silences, and I'm not bothered by any physical distractions that a room might bring — such as dust! In fact, as I observe and enjoy God's creation, I find more things for which to thank and praise Him.

God has called us to come and talk with Him — what an incredible privilege to enter into His presence and dwell there. Come with an open and loving heart, ready to let God set the agenda through His Word and His Spirit. Shut the door behind you — mentally and emotionally, if not physically — and give Him your full attention. Hopefully, as you begin to use these simple suggestions for focusing your attention during prayer, you will experience deeper freedom and joy while dwelling in His presence.

LISTENING TO THE MOST HIGH

Read these prayers of Paul: Ephesians 1:15-18, Ephesians 3:14-20, Philippians 1:9-11, Colossians 1:9-14. How do these prayers encourage you to shut the door and find words for your prayers?

EXPERIENCING HIS POWER AND PRESENCE

As you shut the door and pray in secret, how do you sense the Lord rewarding you?

Write out a verse or two from the Psalms or use one of Paul's prayers and spend some time alone with the Lord interceding for your loved ones.

The soil in which the prayer of faith takes root is a life of unbroken communion with God, a life in which the windows of the soul are always open toward the City of Rest. We do not know the true potency of prayer until our hearts are so intently fixed on God that our thoughts turn to Him whenever they are set free from the consideration of earthly things.[1]

— *David M'Intyre*

Dear Lord, how blessed I am to know that You hear my prayers. Help me to shut the door often so I can grow in knowledge, understanding, and intimacy with You. *Amen.*

ABIDE IN MY WORD

Then Jesus said to those Jews who believed Him, "If you
abide in My word, you are My disciples indeed."

— JOHN 8:31, NKJV

I remember signing up for a calligraphy class offered by our local community college. The classroom was full the first night, and everyone was anticipating learning a new skill. As the class progressed and the assignments became more difficult, attendance began to drop. The last night the teacher commented that we were down to the "faithful few." But she also noted that those of us who completed the course were equipped to enjoy the many facets of calligraphy, and she praised us for our commitment to stay until the very end.

At one point in Jesus' ministry, many of His followers turned away and left Him. These were not true disciples because they did not stay with Jesus. As Jesus watched these disciples go, He turned to the Twelve and asked, "Do you also want to go away?"

(John 6:67, NKJV). Speaking for the Twelve, Peter responded, "Lord, to whom shall we go? You have the words of eternal life. Also we have come to believe and know that You are the Christ, the Son of the living God" (John 6:68-69, NKJV). Peter knew that Jesus was the Truth, the Way, and the Life. He was not leaving; he wanted to stay close and abide with Him.

Because most of the Jews listening to Jesus were antagonistic to Him during this time of teaching in John 8, we can assume that they had only an intellectual belief in the Lord. Jesus needed to give them the test of true discipleship. He addressed those who "believed" in Him by stating that to be an authentic disciple of the Lord, one must abide in His Word. A genuine disciple wants to continue, to stay with, to obey the Word of God.

What does it mean to abide in the Word? For me, *abiding* is consistently sitting at the feet of Jesus with a heart to obey. If I am to continue in the Word, then I must regularly be *in* the Word. A Bible reading plan or a one-year Bible helps me to be faithful. As I have done this over the years, I have discovered that it usually takes about fifteen minutes a day to read the three or four chapters necessary to complete the Bible in a year. Fifteen minutes should fit into anyone's schedule! If I miss a day or two, I usually don't have time to read several days' worth, so I just read the chapters for that day, not worrying about trying to make up the chapters I've missed.

I believe that consistency with the Lord is more important than the length of time spent. Having long, unhurried times with God is special, and certainly this is something we should want to do, but realistically it is not always possible. I believe that fifteen to twenty minutes every day over the years keeps us closer to the Lord than sporadic extended times. And when I read the Word with a heart to obey, this abiding also becomes a time of prayer — for God Himself is speaking to me. In fact, this is the best part of prayer — my listening to the Lord! I have also found that after reading the Word, my prayers are more scriptural and based on the eternal.

The best time to spend with the Lord is early in the morning. David prayed, "My voice You shall hear in the morning, O Lord; in the morning I will direct it to You, and I will look up" (Psalm 5:3, NKJV). The arguments for having quiet times in the morning are obvious — the phone is not ringing, you are not at work, the children are *usually* not up, you are fresh. But the ideal is not always feasible. When I am not able to sit at the feet of the Lord in the morning, then I take my Bible with me and read it whenever I can during the day — during lunch, before I meet someone, before I go to bed. The important thing is not *when* we abide, but that we *do* abide.

Reading through the Bible can be a daunting project. Some passages can be difficult to understand and even harder to apply. God's primary concern, I have come to realize, is not that I understand everything, but that what I do comprehend, I *obey*. Psalm 111:10 confirms this thought: "The fear of the Lord is the beginning of wisdom; a good understanding have all those who do His commandments" (NKJV). The psalmist did not say, "a good understanding have all those who 'know' His commandments." Oswald Chambers wisely taught, "It is not study that does it, but obedience. The tiniest fragment of obedience, and heaven opens and the profoundest truths of God are yours straight away. God will never reveal more truth about Himself until you have obeyed what you know already."[1]

This is the test Jesus gave to those listening to His teaching — the test of obedient abiding. Moffatt translates John 8:31, "If you abide by what I say." The New Living Translation renders, "You are truly my disciples if you remain faithful to my teachings." Staying in the Word with an obedient heart is essential to becoming a faithful follower of Christ.

Jesus, knowing the hearts of those hearing His words, offered this challenge to those who wanted to be a disciple in deed and in truth. The test of a true disciple is steadfastness, commitment, and loyalty to the end. Judas, the one disciple who betrayed Jesus, was not steadfast, loyal, or faithful. He did not remain with Jesus. He did not have an obedient heart. He went through the motions of being with the Lord, but he was not teachable or submissive to the Lord's words.

To be a disciple indeed, it is necessary to abide with a heart to obey. To be an abiding disciple, it is essential to continue with Christ to the end and this blessed commitment is best described as dwelling in His presence.

LISTENING TO THE MOST HIGH

Read John 8:31 and John 15:5. How would you describe the difference between dry observance of religious ritual and a vital "abiding" in Christ?

EXPERIENCING HIS POWER AND PRESENCE

Would you consider yourself to be a disciple "indeed"? Why or why not?

As you spend time before the Lord, ask Him to make you His faithful follower with a heart to obey.

Therefore, my brother, who would learn to abide in Jesus, take time each day, ere you read, and while you read, and after you read, to put yourself into living contact with the living Jesus, to yield yourself distinctly and consciously to His blessed influence; so will you give Him the opportunity of taking hold of you, of drawing you up and keeping you safe in His almighty life.[2]

— Andrew Murray

Father, may I consistently yield myself to your blessed influence and remain Your true disciple. *Amen.*

THE TRUTH WILL SET YOU FREE

And you will know the truth,
and the truth will set you free.

— JOHN 8:32, NLT

A precious woman came and sat down beside me at a conference. With a heavy heart, she told the story of her son who was addicted to cocaine. In fact, at that time, she had no idea where he was. Her last word of him was that he was homeless and destitute but still unwilling to acknowledge that he needed help. How it grieved her to see her son in such bondage, especially when love and support were being offered to help him become free.

"We are descendants of Abraham. . . . We have never been slaves to anyone. What do you mean, 'You will be set free'? . . . We aren't illegitimate children! God himself is our true Father" (John 8:33,41, NLT). These words are a rather hostile response to Jesus' teaching about true discipleship and the power of the truth to give freedom. These Jews felt that since they were Abraham's descendants, they had never been in bondage. They didn't need to be "set free."

The exchange between the Jews and Jesus continued with the Lord telling them that whoever sins is a slave of sin, but if the Son sets you free, you will indeed be free. How could they claim to be children of Abraham? If they were Abraham's offspring, they would love Him and not be seeking to kill Him. Jesus went a step further and declared that they were of their father, the Devil, who was a murderer from the beginning and had no truth in him.

Jesus wanted these Pharisees to understand that they were in bondage to sin and the law. If they would come and abide in His Word, they would know the truth and the truth would set them free. But these dear people said that they were not slaves and certainly had no need of being set free. How tragic to be enslaved and not know it.

I wonder if the future apostle Paul might have been in this group. By his own admission he was "of the stock of Israel, of the tribe of Benjamin, a Hebrew of the Hebrews; concerning the law, a Pharisee; concerning zeal, persecuting the church; concerning the righteousness which is in the law, blameless" (Philippians 3:5-6, NKJV). I'm sure he felt that the Pharisees had a corner on the truth. How dare Jesus say that *He* was the Truth? Since all who believed in Christ were a threat to the Jews, the church needed to be dealt with harshly.

Paul did not think he needed freedom — his heritage and the law made him complete. But a monumental encounter on the road to Damascus dramatically changed Paul's mind and life. Truth Himself confronted this Pharisee of the Pharisees. When he was spiritually blind, he could not see the truth, but in his physical blindness he recognized and embraced the Truth, and he was set free.

Now Paul became zealous for the truth and the freedom that only Christ could bring. He wrote to the Romans, "Once you were slaves of sin, but now you wholeheartedly obey this teaching we have given you. Now you are free from your slavery to sin, and you have become slaves to righteous living" (Romans 6:17-18, NLT).

To be a slave to sin is to habitually practice sin. Concerning those still enslaved, Matthew Henry writes, "He that makes sin, that makes choice of sin, prefers the way of wickedness before the way of holiness . . . they are servants of sin, imprisoned under the guilt of sin, under an arrest, in hold for it, concluded under sin, and they are subject to the power of sin."[1] This enslavement describes the Israelites, who told Jeremiah that they would not listen to God's Word. They preferred to continue burning incense to the Queen of Heaven. Because they chose the way of wickedness, they were not free.

To be a slave to righteousness does not mean that we are sinless. It means that we don't *practice* sin, we don't intend to sin, and we don't make it a habit. When it is brought to our attention, we are repentant.

Once Paul tasted freedom, he zealously preached and guarded this grace that sets prisoners free. Sin destroys and ultimately kills, "but the free gift of God is eternal life through Christ Jesus our Lord" (Romans 6:23, NLT). The freedom that Christ gives enables us, through faith, to become a child of God, to confess our sin, to forgive others, to refrain from practicing sin, to trust God to repay those who hurt us, to rejoice in all that is eternal, to be free from fear, to love God's Word, to hope, and to look forward to a glorious eternity. It keeps us from being enslaved to various man-made spiritual laws that bind and restrict our walk with Christ. Freedom releases burdens, bestows rest, enables obedience, empowers us to love. Freedom is a divine gift from our Savior.

The young son addicted to drugs thinks that he is free — free to make his own choices, free from being tied down to any one or any place, free to go anywhere, free to be his own master. But how could anyone see him and say, "I want the freedom that he has"? For his "freedom" cripples, denies, binds, destroys, humiliates, and keeps him from love, goodness, and peace. He is just like the Pharisees who thought that they were free. At the end of Jesus' conversation with the Jews, they picked up stones to throw at Him. It was all such a paradox. Here were enslaved men thinking they were liberated, throwing rocks to kill the only One who was truly free — the only One who, if they came to know Him, could set them free.

Dear friend, do you know the truth? Have you experienced the freedom that only Christ can give? The blessing of knowing the truth includes the freedom of dwelling in the secret place of the Most High.

LISTENING TO THE MOST HIGH
Read John 8:32. How would you describe the freedom announced in this verse?

EXPERIENCING HIS POWER AND PRESENCE
In what ways do you experience the freedom that only Christ can give?

Spend time in prayer, asking God to reveal to you the ways in which you are most in need of understanding and embracing the truth.

None are free indeed but those whom Christ makes free.[2]
— *Matthew Henry*

Dear Lord, thank You for Your truth that frees me from myself and sin so that I can be a servant in Your kingdom. *Amen.*

KEEP MY COMMANDMENTS

As the Father loved Me, I also have loved you; abide in My love. If you keep My commandments, you will abide in My love, just as I have kept My Father's commandments and abide in His love.

— JOHN 15:9-10, NKJV

He was a man of power. He lived in abundance. He had everything he needed to be content. He even had a heart for God. But one night he stepped away from his relationship with the Lord and committed adultery. In trying to cover up his sin, he resorted to murder. He knew the commandments, but he did not keep them. As a result, he was separated from God and became discouraged and downcast. Listen to his prayer as he describes his feelings:

When I refused to confess my sin, my body wasted away,
and I groaned all day long. Day and night your hand of discipline was heavy on me. My strength evaporated like water
in the summer heat. (Psalm 32:3-4, NLT)

David, the psalmist and king, could testify that disobedience isolates
and oppresses.

The Lord has always been committed to our highest and best.
It is for our benefit that He asks us to obey. Moses encouraged the
Israelites "to keep the commandments of the LORD and His statutes
which I command you today for your good" (Deuteronomy 10:13,
NKJV). Obedience is for our *good,* our protection. Evidence that we
are abiding in Christ's love is our obedience to His commands; we
are secure in His love and free from self. Our concerns are for Him
and His kingdom, not for our own gratification. Disobedience is
costly and destructive. The consequences always outweigh any fleeting pleasure we might experience through sin. The prophet Nathan
announced to David the repercussions of his transgression:

Why, then, have you despised the word of the LORD and done
this horrible deed? For you have murdered Uriah the Hittite
with the sword of the Ammonites and stolen his wife. From
this time on, your family will live by the sword because you
have despised me by taking Uriah's wife to be your own. This
is what the LORD says: Because of what you have done, I will
cause your own household to rebel against you. I will give
your wives to another man before your very eyes, and he will
go to bed with them in public view. (2 Samuel 12:9-11, NLT)

After David expressed his burden of sin in prayer to the Lord, he
wrote, "I acknowledged my sin to You. . . . You forgave the iniquity

of my sin. . . . You are my hiding place; You shall preserve me from trouble; You shall surround me with songs of deliverance" (Psalm 32:5,7, NKJV). Once again David was abiding in His love. There are safety and joy in abiding; there are uncertainty and heartache in separation from the Lord.

The antidote to living with undesirable consequences is choosing to obey the Lord's commands. Jesus makes it as easy as He can for us to obey. First, He says that He loves us in the same way that the Father has loved Him. Christ's love for us corresponds to the Father's love for Him. After the Lord's baptism in the Jordan River, the heavens opened and a voice from heaven said, "This is my dearly loved Son, who brings me great joy" (Matthew 3:17, NLT). In Jesus' prayer to His Father in the garden, He prayed, "I . . . have loved them as You have loved Me" (John 17:23, NKJV). Commentator Albert Barnes observed, "The love of the Father toward his only-begotten Son is the highest affection of which we can conceive."[1] God is Love, so the love shared by the Father and Son is holy, gracious, constant, and complete. It is in this tender, unconditional, and eternal love that our Savior asks that we abide.

This is certainly not an unreasonable request! In fact, it is a gracious invitation to stay close to Him. But just loving the Lord emotionally with no concrete evidence of our love is not enough to keep us abiding. Obedience is a key to abiding and Jesus, Himself, is our model. He said, "For I have come down from heaven, not to do My own will, but the will of Him who sent Me" (John 6:38, NKJV). Paul wrote concerning the incarnation of Jesus, "And being found in appearance as a man, He humbled Himself and became obedient to the point of death, even the death of the cross" (Philippians 2:8, NKJV). Following Jesus' example means obeying the will of God for our lives.

The one all-inclusive command is to love as He has loved us — sacrificially, unconditionally, and selflessly. Jesus told the parable of the good Samaritan in response to the lawyer's question, "And who is my neighbor?" A man was robbed, beaten, and left half-dead on the road. A priest and a Levite passed by on the other side, but a Samaritan stopped to bandage his wounds and take him to an inn. After the Samaritan ministered to him during the night, he left money for his continued care. The Samaritan loved his neighbor — sacrificially, unconditionally, and selflessly.

Since we are fully loved and have the Holy Spirit abiding in us, then we can love and keep His commands. John wrote to the church, "For this is the love of God, that we keep His commandments" (1 John 5:3, NKJV). And His commandments are not burdensome. Jesus taught, "Take my yoke upon you. Let me teach you, because I am humble and gentle at heart, and you will find rest for your souls. For my yoke is easy to bear, and the burden I give you is light" (Matthew 11:29-30, NLT).

It is interesting to consider what we will do to receive love from other people. It affects — and sometimes distorts — the way we dress, speak, and interact. It shapes the work we do, the way we spend our leisure time, the relationships we choose. We will expend and even compromise ourselves in a myriad of ways, desperately trying to get someone to love us. Ultimately, at some point in our lives, we realize that all this performing and maneuvering is for imperfect human love, which cannot completely satisfy. Only the boundless love of Christ can fulfill us. And only through faithfully obeying what He has asked us to do can we experience His love to the fullest. We think that receiving the Lord's love through obedience is a virtually impossible task. In actuality, what is incredibly burdensome is the struggle for temperamental, mortal love.

Because the Lord's love fulfills you and frees you to love others, and because His love allows you to experience Him in greater intimacy, any path that enables you to abide in His love is worth your effort. Obedience in itself is a blessing; but its reward is the intimate and loving presence of Christ Himself.

LISTENING TO THE MOST HIGH

Read John 15:9-10. List some similarities between our abiding in God's love and Jesus' abiding in the Father's love.

EXPERIENCING HIS POWER AND PRESENCE

In what ways does your love for God manifest itself in keeping His commandments?

Draw near to God in prayer, asking Him to lead you into a deeper experience of abiding in His love.

Where there is love to Christ, there is scarcely any need of a command to obey him; but it will follow as the stream from the fountain, or light and heat from the sun.[2]

— *B. Thomas*

Lord, enable me to understand the impact that obedience has on my dwelling in Your presence. *Amen.*

HE WILL GIVE YOU ANOTHER COUNSELOR

And I will ask the Father, and he will give you another Advocate, who will never leave you. He is the Holy Spirit, who leads into all truth. The world cannot receive him, because it isn't looking for him and doesn't recognize him. But you know him, because he lives with you now and later will be in you.

— JOHN 14:16-17, NLT

I was five years old, sitting at the kitchen table, staring at orange carrots on a blue plate. My dad had told me that I could not leave the table until I had eaten these round, cold vegetables. After a period of time, my father said, "If you eat your carrots, I'll take you to a movie." Now it wasn't that I didn't like carrots; for some reason I just didn't want to eat them. Even the inducement of a movie was not enough to motivate me to eat. A little later, he took pity on me and said that I could leave the table. Of course, we didn't go to the movie.

Jesus and the disciples were in the Upper Room where He was giving His final teaching. During their three-year training period, the Lord had been their constant Helper, Comforter, Teacher, Advocate. Now He was telling them that He must leave, but He was not abandoning them or leaving them helpless. He said to them, "If you love me, obey my commandments. And I will ask the Father, and he will give you another Advocate, who will never leave you. He is the Holy Spirit, who leads into all truth" (John 14:15-17, NLT). Through Christ's prayer and the Father's bestowment, another Comforter would be given — not at random, but to those who sincerely followed Christ. Jesus had guided and led the disciples; now the third person of the Trinity would be given to take the place of Jesus. Jesus had related to them by His physical presence; the Holy Spirit would now lead, teach, and comfort them from within.

It is helpful to examine the Holy Spirit's relationship to the Lord Jesus and to the Father. In addressing the disciples, Jesus Himself spoke of the Father and the Holy Spirit — this is a unique sentence, for all three persons of the Trinity are mentioned. Trying to comprehend that God is three in One can be somewhat disconcerting. Martyn Lloyd-Jones comments,

> The Scriptures tell us two great things, first that there
> is only one God. We must always assert that. But the
> Scriptures equally teach that there are three Persons in that
> Godhead — the Father, the Son and the Holy Spirit. God
> the Father is fully God. God the Son is fully God. God the
> Holy Spirit is fully God. Do not try to understand that;

no one can; it baffles our understanding. We must simply come to the Scripture and bow before it, accepting its authority; but we cannot understand it.[1]

Paul wrote to the Romans, "How unsearchable are His judgments and His ways past finding out!" (Romans 11:33, NKJV). Our response to God is grounded in faith.

The Holy Spirit's ministry in our lives is profound, probably more significant than we can ever realize. We are told that at creation, "the Spirit of God was hovering over the face of the waters" (Genesis 1:2, NKJV). Job proclaimed, "The Spirit of God has made me, and the breath of the Almighty gives me life" (Job 33:4, NKJV). Jesus told Nicodemus, "That which is born of the flesh is flesh, and that which is born of the Spirit is spirit" (John 3:6, NKJV); and to others He said, "It is the Spirit who gives life" (John 6:63, NKJV). Jesus referred to the Holy Spirit as the Spirit of truth. The Holy Spirit is the author of all truth. Peter wrote, "No prophecy of Scripture is of any private interpretation, for prophecy never came by the will of man, but holy men of God spoke as they were moved by the Holy Spirit" (2 Peter 1:20-21, NKJV).

The Holy Spirit worked in creation, inspired and controlled the writing of Scripture, is actively at work in our regeneration, and He also spiritually and physically resurrects: "The Spirit of God, who raised Jesus from the dead . . . he will give life to your mortal bodies by this same Spirit living within you" (Romans 8:11, NLT).

The Holy Spirit is a person. "Go therefore and make disciples of all the nations, baptizing them in the name of the Father and of the Son and of the Holy Spirit" (Matthew 28:19, NKJV). He has a will, as Paul indicated when he wrote concerning spiritual gifts, "But one and the same Spirit works all these things, distributing to each one individually as He wills" (1 Corinthians 12:11, NKJV). He also has a mind: "Now He who searches the hearts knows what the mind of the Spirit is, because He makes intercession for the saints according to the will of God" (Romans 8:27, NKJV). The Holy Spirit has emotions: "And do not grieve the Holy Spirit of God, by whom you were sealed for the day of redemption" (Ephesians 4:30, NKJV).

The Spirit of truth intercedes for us and helps in our weaknesses (Romans 8:26-27). He reproves the world: "And when He has come, He will convict the world of sin, and of righteousness, and of judgment" (John 16:8, NKJV). He guides us into all truth (John 16:13, NKJV). The Holy Spirit will testify of Christ and glorify Him (John 15:26; 16:14). He dwells within us: "Don't you realize that your body is the temple of the Holy Spirit, who lives in you and was given to you by God?" (1 Corinthians 6:19, NLT). The Holy Spirit abides in us with the intent of keeping our hearts and minds focused on the Lord Jesus Christ. He does not call attention to Himself, but He works mightily in our lives as our Comforter, Counselor, Helper, and Advocate.

As I consider what my father might have done to persuade me to eat my carrots, I realize that the only way he could have motivated me to obey would have been to enter into my heart somehow and prompt me from within. This is what our heavenly Father has done. When by faith we receive the Lord Jesus Christ as our Savior, we are immediately indwelt by the Holy Spirit, who strengthens us to grow and to obey. What an amazing God we have to come and live in us! Jesus' announcement of the gift of the Holy Spirit is the coming of God's power and presence in our lives.

LISTENING TO THE MOST HIGH
Read John 14:16-17. How do you sense the Holy Spirit's ministry in your life?

EXPERIENCING HIS POWER AND PRESENCE
Describe an area of your life in which you want to be more sensitive to the promptings of the Holy Spirit.

Spend time in prayer, thanking God for the gift of His Holy Spirit.

Let us not only think of what He [the Holy Spirit] does, let us realise who He is. What an act of humiliation and of humbling took place when the Son was born as a babe in Bethlehem! But it is an equal act of humiliation for this third Person in the blessed Trinity to come and to dwell in you and me.[2]

— *Martyn Lloyd-Jones*

Dear Father, I am humbled that Your Spirit lives within me. May I be sensitive to the Spirit's guidance, teaching, comfort, and promptings. *Amen.*

BUT BY MY SPIRIT

*So he answered and said to me: "This is the word of the
LORD to Zerubbabel: 'Not by might nor by power, but by
My Spirit,' says the LORD of hosts."*

— ZECHARIAH 4:6, NKJV

The young teenager brashly proclaimed that he was willing to fight the towering nine-foot giant taunting the armies of the living God. The king tried to discourage the youthful shepherd, but David recounted his victories over a lion and a bear, saying, "The LORD, who delivered me from the paw of the lion and from the paw of the bear, He will deliver me from the hand of this Philistine" (1 Samuel 17:37, NKJV). Spurning the king's armor, David confidently challenged Goliath, claiming that he would triumph because "the LORD rescues his people, but not with sword and spear. This is the LORD's battle, and he will give you to us!" (1 Samuel 17:47, NLT).

Almost five hundred years before the prophet Zechariah penned the above compelling words from the Lord, David staked his life on the trustworthiness of God's power to deliver not by human strength but by His Spirit.

How many times in difficult circumstances I have said, "Only by Your Spirit, Lord!" How many times I have heard others humbly pray, "Not by our might, not by our power, but by Your Spirit, O Lord." This familiar, powerful verse speaks personally to each of us, because life in the world inevitably pits us against fearsome enemies who are bigger and stronger than we are. We know all too well that we cannot possibly prevail with our own resources alone.

Because this verse has meant so much to me, I began to study the circumstances that prompted these comforting words with great anticipation. Do you know why God directed Zechariah to speak to Zerubbabel? Do you even know (or care!) who Zerubbabel was? Read on, because it is a story of God's faithfulness in accomplishing His will among His children.

Israel, chastened by her captivity in Babylon, was released after Cyrus of Persia defeated the Babylonian Empire in 539 BC. A year later, under the leadership of Zerubbabel, the exiles returned to Judah where, with Cyrus's blessing, they began rebuilding the temple. When the foundation was laid, they held a joyful celebration: "With praise and thanks, they sang this song to the LORD: 'He is so good! His faithful love for Israel endures forever!' . . . Many of the older priests, Levites, and other leaders who had seen the first Temple wept aloud when they saw the new Temple's foundation. The others, however, were shouting for joy. The joyful shouting and weeping mingled together in a loud noise that could be heard far in the distance" (Ezra 3:11-13, NLT). The return to Jerusalem and the reconstruction of the temple were an overwhelming joy to these exiles, because it was truly a homecoming. Solomon's temple had been destroyed fifty years earlier, and the old men who remembered the splendor of the earlier temple were overcome with emotion.

Their joy was fleeting, however. Opposition to the building imme-diately sprang up in the form of the local residents, the Samaritans. These "neighbors" tried to frighten, discourage, and hinder the Israelites from their work. They bribed officials and wrote accusatory letters to the king. Finally, after many years, the Persian king Artaxerxes issued an order for the rebuilding to stop. Later, King Darius lifted the restric-tions, but the people had lost their earlier zeal, and they abandoned the work on the temple and concentrated instead on building their own homes. It was easy for them to procrastinate working on the temple, for it never seemed to be the right time to begin again.

By the year 520 BC, sixteen years had elapsed since any labor had been done on the temple. The exiles were selfishly consumed with their own welfare rather than sacrificially concerned about the temple. To the Lord, the temple represented their meeting together; it was a symbol of His abiding presence. Even though God sought to get their attention through drought and economic difficulties, the people were oblivious to His chastening through these trials. Therefore, it became necessary for God to send His prophets Haggai and Zechariah to confront and encourage the Israelites to repent and recognize their lack of spiritual priorities. Haggai spoke for the Lord, "'Why are you living in luxurious houses while my house lies in ruins? . . . Look at what's happening to you! . . . Now go up into the hills, bring down timber, and rebuild my house. Then I will take pleasure in it and be honored, says the LORD" (Haggai 1:4-5,8, NLT).

Zerubbabel, Joshua (the high priest), and all the people heard and obeyed the voice of the Lord. Assured of the Lord's presence and help, they began rebuilding the temple in earnest. But as soon as construction began, so did resistance. Tattenai, a regional governor, protested their renewed work by sending a letter of protest to King Darius. Doubtless Zerubbabel experienced discouragement when he encountered opposition yet again.

This is when Zechariah had a vision of a solid gold lampstand flanked by two olive trees. He asked the angel who had awakened him to this vision and what it all meant. The angel replied, "This is the word of the LORD to Zerubbabel: 'Not by might nor by power, but by My Spirit,' says the LORD of hosts. 'Who are you, O great mountain? Before Zerubbabel you shall become a plain! And he shall bring forth the capstone with shouts of "Grace, grace to it!"'" (Zechariah 4:6-7, NKJV). The essence of the vision was to affirm to Zerubbabel that the temple would be built by a continual supply of the oil of grace, which represented the Holy Spirit. Zerubbabel did not have to depend on human strength or force to accomplish his task. The temple would be erected by the power of the Spirit, and therefore he did not need to fear any adversary.

The Lord reassured Zerubbabel that any resistance or difficulties he might encounter would be removed — any mountains would be leveled. Zerubbabel had laid the foundation of the temple, and he would also finish it. What might seem impossible to man was possible with God, because the Holy Spirit has power and might to accomplish all of God's purposes. Through the work of the Spirit, Darius ordered Tattenai not to hinder the building — in fact, he was to be sure that the Jews had everything they needed to complete the temple, which was finished with much joy in 515 BC.

These tender words of comfort to Zerubbabel are also God's loving words to us. When we are in the center of God's will, carrying out His purposes for our lives, we can be assured that any mountains or giants we face can be overcome not by our own effort, but by the power of the Holy Spirit. Paul's words to the Philippians confirm this truth: "Being confident of this very thing, that He who has begun a good work in you will complete it until the day of Jesus Christ" (Philippians 1:6, NKJV). God is the One who brings to completion His work in our lives. Our part is to cooperate with Him, to be obedient and available for Him to use so we can participate in and experience His marvelous grace, power, and presence. On this basis we can confidently "build" each day, resting in the certainty of His Spirit to go before us.

LISTENING TO THE MOST HIGH

Read Zecharaiah 4:6. What are some other examples from the Scriptures of how people accomplished the seemingly impossible because of the enabling power of the Holy Spirit?

EXPERIENCING HIS POWER AND PRESENCE

What "mountain" are you facing, which you know can be climbed only by the power of the Holy Spirit?

As you come to the Lord in prayer, thank Him for His might and power and ask Him to encourage your heart that He is with you and will never leave or forsake you.

Zerubbabel, in rebuilding the temple, had enormous difficulties. Those difficulties hovered before him as mountains. But great as they were, he was assured that he had resources more than equal to the task. . . . The difficulties in a good man's path of duty rise often-times like mountains before him; but let him not be disheartened; those mountains are nothing compared with the might that is guaranteed.[1]

—*D. Thomas*

Dear Father, help me to remember that it is only by Your power, Your might, and Your spirit that Your purposes are fulfilled. *Amen.*

LOOK FOR THE ANCIENT PATHS

*These are the words of the LORD: Stop at the cross-roads;
look for the ancient paths; ask, "Where is the way that
leads to what is good?" Then take that way, and you will
find rest for yourselves. But they said, "We will not."*

— JEREMIAH 6:16, NEB

It was my first time in England. I was with a dear friend who had lived in Oxford for a year, and she was excited about showing me her adopted country. She drove, and I navigated. One particular day we were driving in Manchester, looking for an old mansion. Since I was in charge of figuring out how to get to our destination, it was my responsibility to ask for directions. We must have stopped at least five or six times to inquire about the way to Lyme Hall. Some people were very specific about which routes to take; others were rather vague. I soon learned that older people, the ones who had most likely lived there the longest, were the best sources for the clearest and most definite directions.

Before the Lord gave these words of counsel through Jeremiah about inquiring for the good way, He observed, "But my people have stubborn and rebellious hearts . . . the prophets give false prophecies, and the priests rule with an iron hand. Worse yet, my people like it that way! . . . They scorn the word of the LORD" (Jeremiah 5:23,31; 6:10, NLT). When God exhorted His children to stop at the crossroads and ask for the good, old paths, it was a final plea for them to turn from their rebellion, to seek what is right and find rest. These words carry a keen sense of God's longing for His people to stop, look, and consider what they were doing — to count the cost of the results if they continued on their chosen path. He wanted peace and security for them, but they were headed for upheaval and exile. Jeremiah told Judah, "The LORD of Heaven's Armies, the God of Israel, says: 'Even now, if you quit your evil ways, I will let you stay in your own land'" (Jeremiah 7:3, NLT). If only you would stand still and see what your options are. Ask for the proven way that leads to rest — at least stop and ask!

The Jews had forsaken the old ways. Listen to the Lord's words to them: "Do you really think you can steal, murder, commit adultery, lie, and burn incense to Baal and all those other new gods of yours, and then come here and stand before me in my Temple and chant, 'We are safe!' — only to go right back to all those evils again?" (Jeremiah 7:9-10, NLT). Certainly one clear way that had been given to Israel was "*do not* steal, murder, commit adultery, lie, and worship other gods." But they turned away from this good, ancient path their Father had lovingly entrusted to them. Not only had they rebelled by adding new gods, they blatantly entered the temple and went through the pretense of worshiping God. How patient the Lord was to ask that Judah stop, look, and listen.

"*Stop where you are and see!*" — stand still and give thoughtful consideration to your choices. It's been said that we are free to choose where we want to go, but we are not free to choose the consequences of that choice. The prodigal son chose to take his inheritance and live selfishly. When he was destitute, he finally stopped and saw where he was — a hog pen! "He finally came to his senses," Luke says (15:17, NLT). This is what God wanted Judah to do — stop, see where they were, and come to their senses!

Look for the ancient paths; ask, "Where is the way that leads to what is good?" It is the old, well-worn path we should be looking for. My husband and I recently hiked up to a beautiful waterfall, which required a rigorous climb. It was evident that countless people had gone before us, for the path was well-worn. As we met others coming down from the falls, we asked, "Is it worth the climb?" They inevitably replied, "Oh, yes! Just keep going on the path." This is the "asking" that God wants all His children to do. We are to look for the ancient path — the tried-and-true way, which others have traveled who can affirm to us, "This is the way that leads to what is good."

The prodigal son wanted to leave, but he did not ask directions to the good, old path. Rather, he chose a path that Proverbs 14:12 warns about: "There is a path before each person that seems right, but it ends in death" (NLT). If we don't stop and consider, seeking counsel for the good way, our path may lead us to "dine with swine."

Not all old paths are good, however, and neither are all new paths wrong. I like this commentator's insight: "In these new ways what is true will be found to be old. . . . All the 'old' paths are not also 'good ways'; far from it. But there is an old, and therefore well-known, well-trodden, and hence unmistakable way, which also is the *good* way."[1] Solomon wisely wrote, "That which has been is what will be, that which is done is what will be done, and there is nothing new under the sun. Is there anything of which it may be said, 'See, this is new'?" (Ecclesiastes 1:9-10, NKJV).

Concerning reading what is new, C. S. Lewis wrote,

It is a good rule, after reading a new book, never to allow yourself another new one until you have read an old one in between . . . the only palliative is to keep the clean sea breeze of the centuries blowing through our minds, and this can be done only by reading old books.[2]

The path that is paved with truth and leads to goodness is the path that Jesus trod. Jesus emphatically proclaimed, "I am the way, the truth, and the life. No one can come to the Father except through me" (John 14:6, NLT). The only path worth choosing is the eternal path that leads to God. The only path that offers rest is the one to His heart.

The tragedy of these precious words from our heavenly Father is that Judah did not stop and ask for the ancient, good path; she did not choose rest. In fact, her response to God was, "We will not." We can read these verses and think, *How foolish to go down a path that leads to heartache and exile. How absurd to turn your back on God.* But are we not the same? We, too, stand at the crossroads: in one direction we see a wide, smooth path ahead that promises pleasure and all that we desire from this world; in the other we see a path that looks well-traveled, but it is narrow, a little rocky, and removed from the world. The sign at the first road reads, "To the New and Easy." The sign at the second path reads, "To the Ancient and True." God says, "Stop at the crossroads and look around. Ask for the old, godly way, and walk in it. Travel its path, and you will find rest for your souls" (Jeremiah 6:16, NLT).

LISTENING TO THE MOST HIGH

Read Jeremiah 6:16. How does following "the way that leads to what is good" lead to rest, and departing from it lead to unrest?

EXPERIENCING HIS POWER AND PRESENCE

How can the good, ancient path give you rest?

Spend time in prayer, asking God to reveal to you the crossroads in your life where you have opportunity to choose what is right.

It is the "old way." New as regards the light Christianity has shed upon it, new as regards the revelation of him in whose redeeming work its deep foundations have been laid, it is "old" as regards its essential principles of faith and righteousness. The martyrs, prophets, and holy men of every age have left their glowing footprints upon it.[3]

—*J. Waite*

Dear Father, thank You for the proven path that is easily discernible, if I will but stop and see. *Amen.*

KEEP THEM FROM THE EVIL ONE

I do not pray that You should take them out of the world,
but that You should keep them from the evil one.

— JOHN 17:15, NKJV

"Cynthia Ann, don't ever let a stranger come into our home!" My mother spoke these words to me more than fifty years ago. I had invited a door-to-door portrait salesman to come into our living room. He asked if we had ever had a photographer take a formal portrait. I was very proud of a picture taken of me for my piano recital, so I thought he should see it. When my mother heard voices, she was shocked to see a strange man in our home. After he left, I received her strong warning.

Parents are responsible for protecting and training their children to be wise in relating to people and the world around them. Today there are books for children to read about speaking to strangers. Schools conduct role-playing exercises to help children know what to do in potentially dangerous circumstances. Our world is not always a safe place, and we must learn to be on guard.

Despite the chaotic and dangerous condition of the world, in His prayer of intercession for all believers, Jesus prayed that we would not be taken out of this environment. Even though we are not *of* the world as His children, we need to be *in* the world as salt and light to those who do not believe in Christ. This world is fundamentally unreceptive and antagonistic to the gospel because it is under Satan's dominion. The apostle John wrote, "We know that we are children of God and that the world around us is under the control of the evil one" (1 John 5:19, NLT). Since we live in a world exploited by Satan, Jesus lovingly intercedes for our safekeeping from the evil one.

I think it is significant that Jesus prayed, "keep them from the evil one," not "keep the evil one from them." Satan is here in our midst by permission, and he will not be removed until God so designates. In His sovereignty, God has given Satan full reign for a season and allows him to test His children. Job is a prime example. God brought Job to Satan's attention and then gave the evil one freedom to test Job's character: "Then the LORD said to Satan, 'Have you considered My servant Job, that there is none like him on the earth. . . . Behold, all that he has is in your power" (Job 1:8,12, NKJV). Another example can be found in Jesus' words to Peter: "Simon, Simon! Indeed, Satan has asked for you, that he may sift you as wheat. But I have prayed for you, that your faith should not fail; and when you have returned to Me, strengthen your brethren" (Luke 22:31-32, NKJV). Jesus did not pray for Satan to be kept from Peter; instead, He prayed that Peter's faith would withstand Satan's sifting.

Jesus' words to the church in Smyrna also reveal how Satan is allowed to attack believers: "Do not fear any of those things which you are about to suffer. Indeed, the devil is about to throw some of you into prison, that you may be tested, and you will have tribulation ten days. Be faithful until death, and I will give you the crown of life" (Revelation 2:10, NKJV). Again, the Lord did not pray for Satan to be kept from the believers; He encourages His children to persevere, to be steadfast and strengthened in their spirits. Since Satan is a given in our world, it does not make sense to expend energy trying to pray him away or battle with him, apart from the ways God employs for us to be safe inwardly from his attacks.

God seems to place a higher priority on our spiritual safety than on our physical well-being. At the end of his trial, Job humbly proclaimed, "I had only heard about you before, but now I have seen you with my own eyes" (Job 42:5, NLT). After Satan's sifting, Peter returned to the Lord and then strengthened his brethren in leading the early church. Jesus was concerned that the believers in Smyrna remain to the very end faithful witnesses of their love for Christ. The Lord wants us to stand our ground with Satan while we are here, courageously trusting in God's strength to withstand his assaults.

As our heavenly parent, God equips us in how to stand firm against Satan's attacks, for in resisting Satan our faith is strengthened and perfected. It pleases our Father when we recognize evil and choose to turn away from it. For our defense, He has provided spiritual armor, as Paul explained to the Ephesians: "Put on the whole armor of God, that you may be able to stand against the wiles of the devil" (Ephesians 6:11, NKJV).

The first piece of armor Paul mentioned is the *belt of truth*. One of Satan's ploys is to cast doubt on the truth of God's Word, as he did with Eve: "Has God indeed said?" (Genesis 3:1, NKJV). Jesus is the truth; therefore, abiding in Him and His Word enables us to be girded with truth.

When Joseph was enticed by Potiphar's wife, he was able to flee from her presence because he had on the *breastplate of righteousness,* the second piece of armor.

The *gospel of peace* is for our feet, leading us not into wickedness but into sharing the good news of reconciliation as we fulfill our calling to be ambassadors for Christ.

Jesus prayed that Peter's faith would hold — it was the *shield of faith,* which quenches the evil one's fiery darts, that Peter needed when he was sifted by Satan. Faith enables us to resist and to stand firm.

The *helmet of salvation* is for the most vulnerable part of our body. A blow to the head, if not fatal, can cause disorientation and confusion. Confidence in our salvation and in our Savior keeps us clear-headed and alert.

The *sword of the Spirit* is the Word of God, which we are to take up and use proactively in our battle with the enemy. Jesus modeled this use when He countered Satan's temptations with "It is written . . ." (Matthew 4:4, NKJV).

Clothing ourselves with the armor of God empowers us to resist Satan to the point that he will flee from us (James 4:7). Truly, the armor enables us to be steadfast and secure against the enemy of our souls. How do we know that we are fully armored? For me, it is in abiding that I know and am confident that I have the whole armor of God. If I sit daily at the Lord's feet, I am strengthened in my spirit — as I learn His truth, my faith grows and I become more proficient in using His Word.

If you are God's child and are dwelling in His presence, then you can be confident that Christ's loving prayer is being answered in your life — the power of His presence will keep your spirit safe from the evil one.

LISTENING TO THE MOST HIGH
Read John 17:15. What are some of the perils of living in the world, for which we need the Father's protection?

EXPERIENCING HIS POWER AND PRESENCE
What are the ways in which you put on the full armor of God to protect yourself against Satan's attacks?

As you spend time in prayer, thank the Lord for the gracious provision He has made for keeping you safe from the evil one.

There is no real and ultimate advantage in a mechanical or artificial diminution of evil, and strategic victory over the evil one. He will only gather his forces and rush out with greater vehemence and success. The policy of our great General was to let him have fair play . . . then let him be conquered under these circumstances. The victory is final, complete, and most glorious.[1]

— B. Thomas

Dear Lord, may I stand firm in the power of Your armor while I am in this world. *Amen.*

FEAR ONLY GOD

Don't be afraid of those who want to kill your body;
they cannot touch your soul. Fear only God,
who can destroy both soul and body in hell.

— MATTHEW 10:28, NLT

In 1899, the Boxer movement began in China as a secret society devoted to the overthrow of the Qing dynasty and the extermination of foreigners. But the Dowager Empress cleverly manipulated the Boxers to concentrate only on eliminating foreigners, most of whom were missionaries. In their zeal, the fanatical Boxers targeted not only missionaries but also Chinese converts as well. I was deeply touched as I read the following account in an overseas missionary fellowship newsletter:

The wife of Mr. Chang was taken to a place where not far away were the corpses of about seven Chinese Christians who had been hacked to pieces. She thought, "This is one of the places where they kill the Christians, and I am going to be killed. O Lord Jesus, give me courage to witness for Thee until the end." The Boxer who had brought her there said, "Are you a Christian?" She replied, "I am." He then placed a stick of incense in her hand and said, "Burn this to the gods and your life will be saved." She replied firmly, "Never." The crowd who had gathered round began to jeer and laugh, and said, "Kill her, kill her, and see if her body will rise again and go to Jesus Christ!" She turned upon them and said, "My body cut in pieces will remain scattered on the ground as these others, but my spirit will escape you and rise to God." She heard the soldiers exclaim, "How bold she is! She is not a bit afraid to die!"[1]

Mrs. Chang was a bold and courageous martyr as she triumphantly fulfilled Jesus' words not to fear those who can destroy the body. She knew that the only power these soldiers had over her was physical. Her soul, her innermost being, was secure with God. She would not burn incense to an idol, for she feared and reverenced God alone as the One who had power over both body and soul.

When Jesus sent out the twelve disciples on their first missionary journey, He prepared them with a realistic warning of the persecution they would face. The disciples were commissioned to preach and teach as they had been taught: "What I tell you now in the darkness, shout abroad when daybreak comes. What I whisper in your ear, shout from the housetops for all to hear!" (Matthew 10:27, NLT). In boldly proclaiming the gospel and identifying with Christ, they would encounter opposition. They were not to be surprised at any mistreatment, because a disciple is not above his teacher. Since Jesus had been and would be condemned, the Twelve should expect the same response from the world. Therefore, they were not to fear anyone — because man's power to destroy is limited only to what is temporal. The physical body, which will fade away, is a small matter in relation to our soul, which will live forever. Paul had this very perspective when he wrote during a period of great persecution, "Though our bodies are dying, our spirits are being renewed every day" (2 Corinthians 4:16, NLT).

With this perspective in mind, Jesus told His disciples who it was they should truly fear: the One "who is able to destroy both soul and body in hell" (Matthew 10:28, NKJV). Only God can condemn a soul to hell, so God is to be feared instead of man. Matthew Henry's insight helps explain Jesus' warning: "The soul is killed when it is separated from God and his love, which is its life."[2] This knowledge of the awesome power of God must have motivated the disciples to be even more diligent in preaching the gospel.

God is almighty, and we are to revere Him for the salvation He offers for souls, and to fear Him for His ability to judge and punish. Paul wrote to the Thessalonians, "And God will provide rest for you who are being persecuted and also for us when the Lord Jesus appears from heaven. He will come with his mighty angels, in flaming fire, bringing judgment on those who don't know God and on those who refuse to obey the Good News of our Lord Jesus. They will be punished with eternal destruction, forever separated from the Lord and from his glorious power" (2 Thessalonians 1:7-9, NLT). Those who turn away from God will experience eternal death; those who receive Him will be granted eternal life.

After this sober warning about God's justice, Jesus comforted His disciples with the tender compassion of the Father. Even though sparrows are so abundant that their value is minuscule, God still knows when one of them falls. God's providential care extends to knowing the most intimate details about His children, such as the number of hairs on their heads. If God cares this much about His creation, then we can be certain He knows and is watchful over all that happens to His own. We can be free from fearing people because we are of such high value to God.

Our hallowed fear of God gives us peace and freedom from every other kind of fear. Daniel epitomized the freedom that comes from honoring and revering God. Despite the plot devised by the jealous governors, Daniel defied the statute of worshiping only the king by continuing to pray and give thanks to his God. He feared neither men nor the certain death his worship would bring. Mrs. Chang experienced that same freedom and security. The question that King Darius posed to Daniel could be asked of this dear Chinese saint: "Mrs. Chang, servant of the living God! Was your God, whom you worship continually, able to rescue you from the lions?" Although the outcome of their courage and trust in God was different, her answer would be the same as Daniel's — a resounding and glorious "Yes!"

LISTENING TO THE MOST HIGH

Read Matthew 10:28. How would you describe the differences between these two kinds of fear: (1) of those who can destroy the body, and (2) of the One who can destroy both body and soul?

EXPERIENCING HIS POWER AND PRESENCE

What earthly fears can you let go of, in response to these words in Matthew 10 from Jesus?

Ask the Lord to grant you a holy fear that casts out all other fears.

But there is a holy fear . . . which is the beginning of wisdom . . . which casts out all other fears — the fear of God. The power of the persecutors is but for a moment. His is the kingdom and the power and the glory for ever and ever. . . . This is not the fear which hath torment. It is not a slavish fear; it is that deep, loving reverence which gives true dignity to the Christian life.[3]

— *B. C. Caffin*

Father, may my life reflect a loving reverence that will free me to be a courageous witness. *Amen.*

DO NOT FEAR THE REPROACH OF MEN

Listen to Me, you who know righteousness, you people in whose heart is My law: Do not fear the reproach of men, nor be afraid of their insults.

— ISAIAH 51:7, NKJV

On a plane, I was sitting next to a man who noticed that I was reading my Bible. He eventually asked, "Do you really believe everything in that book?" I inwardly cringed and prayed. I am not ashamed of the gospel, but I do not welcome controversial exchanges. I don't like to be the object of ridicule or criticism, and I wasn't sure if his question was motivated by hostility or curiosity. The memory flashed across my mind of a time when another stranger had asked me a similar question, and our conversation centered around whether Jonah could have survived inside a whale.

I admit that I can be fearful of what others might say in such encounters. This is why Isaiah 51:7 is a loving word from God to my heart.

This word came through the prophet Isaiah to Israel when they were being taunted by the Babylonians. To comfort His children, God spoke directly to the faithful remnant — to those who followed after righteousness, seeking the Lord. He assured them that His righteousness was near: "My mercy and justice are coming soon. My salvation is on the way. My strong arm will bring justice to the nations" (Isaiah 51:5, NLT). This is the context in which the Lord addressed a weakness that those who know Him and love His Word might have: the fear of men. The writer of Proverbs tells us, "The fear of man brings a snare, but whoever trusts in the LORD shall be safe" (Proverbs 29:25, NKJV). Being afraid of people takes away our freedom and peace. This fear entraps us, and subtlety keeps us from being bold. If we love righteousness and have His Word in our hearts, most likely, at some time in our lives, we might find ourselves defending Jonah's experience.

Jesus encountered the reproach of men. The Pharisees tested Him and plotted against Him in every way they could — ultimately rejoicing in His death. The Lord spoke prophetically of this condemnation in Isaiah: "I gave My back to those who struck Me, and My cheeks to those who plucked out the beard; I did not hide My face from shame and spitting" (50:6, NKJV). The apostles met reproach when they were arrested for preaching. They were beaten, but "they departed from the presence of the council, rejoicing that they were counted worthy to suffer shame for His name" (Acts 5:41, NKJV). God prepared Jeremiah to expect reproach, warning him when he was about to begin his ministry, "'They will fight against you, but they shall not prevail against you. For I am with you,' says the LORD, 'to deliver you'" (Jeremiah 1:19, NKJV).

Through Isaiah, God emphatically tells us not to fear men — and in His next breath He tells us why: those who slander and ridicule His children will be like garments eaten by moths or like wool that is consumed by worms (Isaiah 51:8). Matthew Henry comments, "The matter is not great what those say of us who must shortly be food for worms.... The falsehood of their reproaches will be detected, but truth shall triumph."[1] These are men who will give an account of their lives and words to the living God. They will have to answer for their derisive attitudes. Psalm 1 calls the man "blessed" who does not sit in the seat of the scornful (verse 1, NKJV).

This instruction not to fear reproof is given to those who specifically know the Lord and cherish His Word in their hearts. David reflected on the results the righteous can suffer: "The godly offer good counsel; they teach right from wrong. They have made God's law their own, so they will never slip from his path. The wicked wait in ambush for the godly, looking for an excuse to kill them. But the LORD will not let the wicked succeed or let the godly be condemned when they are put on trial" (Psalm 37:30-33, NLT).

Jesus taught all His disciples how to respond to persecution: "God blesses you when people mock you and persecute you and lie about you and say all sorts of evil things against you because you are my followers. Be happy about it! Be very glad! For a great reward awaits you in heaven" (Matthew 5:11-12, NLT). This all seems so contradictory — rejoice when persecuted, misunderstood, wrongly accused. For me, this is one of those teachings that is easier said than done.

But God prefaces His command not to fear man by addressing those who know righteousness and who have His law abiding in their hearts. Perhaps this is the key to being unafraid of reproach — preferring God's way and approval more than people's acceptance. Dwelling in His presence and abiding in the security of God's Word, we become zealous for what is right — willingly and joyfully suffering reproach if need be. Are we like the disciples, so in love with the Lord that we rejoice in being counted worthy to suffer shame for His name?

"Do you believe everything in the Bible?"

"Why, yes, actually I do. As a matter of fact, I even believe that Jonah lived for three days in the belly of the whale."

LISTENING TO THE MOST HIGH

Read Isaiah 51:7. Why do you think this encouragement to be unafraid of criticism is directed to those who know and love God?

EXPERIENCING HIS POWER AND PRESENCE

Can you recall an incident in which you were anxious or afraid of "the reproach of men"? How did you respond and why?

Confess to God any fear you have of being criticized by others for your faith and spend time listening to His words to you through this passage in Isaiah.

If the praise of man elates me and his blame depresses me; if I cannot rest under misunderstanding without defending myself; if I love to be loved more than to love, to be served more than to serve, then I know nothing of Calvary love.[2]

— Amy Carmichael

Dear Lord, free me from my people-pleasing tendency and may I learn to rejoice whenever I'm misunderstood or judged for my faith. *Amen.*

LOVE ME MORE THAN . . .

A large crowd was following Jesus. He turned around and said to them, "If you want to be my disciple, you must hate everyone else by comparison — your father and mother, wife and children, brothers and sisters — yes, even your own life. Otherwise, you cannot be my disciple."

— LUKE 14:25-26, NLT

I listened as a dear friend described her joy in having her family nearby. All of her children and grandchildren live here in Tucson, and she is blessed to be able to visit, baby-sit, and have special family gatherings for birthdays and holidays on a regular basis. Her life is filled with being a mother and grandmother.

As I left her, I felt a little lonely and deprived. All four of our children are permanently settled far away from Tucson. As I spoke to the Lord about my longings to be more involved with my family, He gently whispered these thoughts to my heart: *Cynthia, you are where you need to be, and your children are where they need to be. I have some specific purposes for you to accomplish at this time in your life and in order for you to fulfill them, you do not have the time for the added involvement that your family would require. You are not to compare the ministry I have given you with the ministry I have given to your friend. Remember, if you are My disciple, you are to love Me more than anyone else.*

I meet many women who are privileged to have their families nearby and are able to be a part of their parents' and children's lives. These women are no less Christ's disciples, for proximity to or distance from our families does not determine our commitment as a disciple. It is the attitude of our hearts that Jesus addresses: Whom do we love the most? Each of us must answer and respond to His teaching in different ways — some by living close to family, some by living far away.

On His final journey to Jerusalem, Jesus was accompanied by a multitude of people. Some sincerely wanted to hear the truth; some were only curious; some were fascinated by His miraculous works; some were truly skeptical. It was time for the Lord to speak in realistic terms about the cost of following Him. He needed to dispel any romantic notions about what was required of His disciples. In enticing his followers, the enemy declares only the benefits of yielding to his way. Satan did this to Eve — "You won't die! . . . You will be like God, knowing both good and evil" (Genesis 3:4-5, NLT). In contrast, Jesus spoke strongly and honestly about true discipleship.

Because of Jesus' miraculous healings and constant concern for the lost and poor, surely some of the people expected Him to promise continual blessing and well-being to His disciples. As Matthew Henry commented, "They expected that he should say, 'If any man come to me, and be my disciple, he shall have wealth and honour in abundance.'"[1] In contrast, instead of promising favor and privilege, Jesus demands something from His followers — first place in their deepest affections. His call is to love Him more than family or self. To be Christ's disciple, loyalty and love for Him are the highest priority.

When He sent out the twelve disciples, Jesus told them,

> Don't imagine that I came to bring peace to the earth! I
> came not to bring peace, but a sword. "I have come to set
> a man against his father, a daughter against her mother,
> and a daughter-in-law against her mother-in-law. Your
> enemies will be right in your own household!" (Matthew
> 10:34-36, NLT)

Jesus wanted His disciples to expect that following Him might result in opposition from those closest to them. Choosing to be Christ's disciple can bring pain and heartache within a family — so in order to be a faithful follower, one must be devoted to Jesus wholeheartedly.

Scripture records a disciple approaching Jesus and asking permission to bury his father before following the Lord. This disciple's father was not dead, but his request was to go and live at home until his father died — his possible motive was to be able to receive his inheritance. Jesus responded by saying, "Follow Me, and let the dead bury their own dead" (Matthew 8:22, NKJV). Family circumstances should not determine discipleship.

In the 1930s, Isobel Kuhn and her husband were sent as missionaries to the Lisu tribe on the China-Burma border. As a young woman Isobel felt called to China, but her mother, although a Christian, was opposed to her going overseas. As much as Isobel loved her mother and desired to honor her, she knew that her higher call was to obey the Lord. Trusting God to go before her, Isobel stepped out in faith and began to make the necessary preliminary plans to study at Moody Bible Institute, which was her first step in going to China. Isobel's trust was rewarded, and she received her mother's reluctant permission to go to Chicago. I read the story of Isobel Kuhn more than twenty years ago, but I have never forgotten her commitment to follow Christ and to trust Him in the midst of family resistance.

The widow Ruth proved her willingness to love God more than her mother, father, and family when she left Moab to live in Bethlehem with Naomi. When Abraham was willing to sacrifice Isaac, he demonstrated that he loved God more than his own son. Countless Christian martyrs have testified that their own lives were expendable in light of knowing and obeying Christ.

Several years ago, I had my conversation with the Lord about not having any family nearby. This past summer our eldest daughter, whose husband is in the Air Force, called from Korea to tell us that they were being stationed in Tucson. At first I thought this could not be true; we had all been praying for England! Never in my wildest imagination did I even consider the possibility of their being near us for an assignment. As I went to the Lord, I said, "I can't believe it! Only You could arrange this!" The Lord graciously answered, *Cynthia, loving Me more than your family doesn't mean that you have to give them up. It does mean that when you love Me with all your heart and you willingly surrender your life to Me, then you are able to love them with My love, and I am able to bless you in surprising ways.*

LISTENING TO THE MOST HIGH

Read Luke 14:25-26. List some specific examples of situations to which these words of Jesus apply.

EXPERIENCING HIS POWER AND PRESENCE

In what sense might God be asking you to make a higher priority of your love for Him than your love for family or friends?

Spend time in prayer asking God to reveal to you how these words from Jesus speak to your heart today.

Nothing is fairer, finer, more beautiful in human life than love of father, and mother, and wife, and children, and brothers and sisters. Yet these fair things may, and often do, challenge our loyalty to our Lord. [If ever] there is a conflict between the call of the highest earthly love and the call of Christ . . . [we] must trample across our own hearts and go after Him, without any compromise and any questionings.[2]

— Amy Carmichael

Dear Lord, may You always be my first love. *Amen.*

SET YOURSELVES APART TO BE HOLY

So set yourselves apart to be holy, for I am the LORD your
God. Keep all my decrees by putting them into practice,
for I am the LORD who makes you holy.

— LEVITICUS 20:7-8, NLT

Many years ago God impressed on me His desire for holiness. I was reading in 1 Peter when these verses leaped out at me:

> But now you must be holy in everything you do, just as God who chose you is holy. For the Scriptures say, "You must be holy because I am holy." (1 Peter 1:15-16, NLT)

God's teaching could not have been clearer. As a relatively new disciple, I cried out to God asking how I could possibly be holy in everything I did. A little while later, while reading in

Leviticus, I found some insight into living a holy life.

In Leviticus 20:7, God asks that we set ourselves apart. This means stepping away from the world's influence. Jesus asked this in His prayer to the Father: "I'm not asking you to take them out of the world, but to keep them safe from the evil one. They do not belong to this world any more than I do. Make them holy by your truth; teach them your word, which is truth" (John 17:15-17, NLT). Paul wrote to Titus that God's desire for His people's holiness is why Jesus gave Himself for us, "that He might redeem us from every lawless deed and purify for Himself His own special people, zealous for good works" (Titus 2:14, NKJV). Jesus came to redeem us so that we become His particular children — so that although we live in the world, we can be like Him — pure and holy.

I remember being told as a new Christian that anyone meeting me should sense something different in my life. Once we are the Lord's, we should become distinctive from people in general, because we are set apart from other people. We "turn from godless living and sinful pleasures. We should live in this evil world with wisdom, righteousness, and devotion to God" (Titus 2:12, NLT). The difference others should see in us is Christ — the presence of holiness.

When God gave these instructions in Leviticus to Moses, He had very specific and precise laws the Israelites were to live by. How do we, today, set ourselves apart?

I find that "consecrating" myself to holiness involves not so much denying myself sinful pleasures as choosing to enjoy that which is true, honorable, right, lovely, and admirable — the qualities we are asked to dwell on in Philippians 4:8. Pursuing holiness does not mean living a dismal life. There is much that is lovely and admirable in classic literature, film, and music. But I have found that to develop the inclination to choose what is true and honorable, it is necessary to decide, first, that holiness is the path I want to take.

Oswald Chambers counseled, "The battle is lost or won in the secret places of the will before God, never first in the external world. . . . Get alone with God, fight it out before Him, settle the matter there once and for all."[1] I remember bowing before the Lord and telling Him that I wanted to live as holy a life as I could. It was a simple transaction made between the Father and His child. Since then I certainly have not been perfect, but at that time I set my heart to travel on the highway of holiness.

We are to set ourselves apart not because a set of rules for prescribed behavior has been handed down to us, but because the Lord is our God and He is holy. As people who reflect His presence and power, we will reflect His holiness. God is our Father, and He would like His children to have some family resemblance!

When Isaiah experienced his magnificent vision of God seated on His throne, he heard the seraphim cry out, "Holy, holy, holy is the LORD of Heaven's Armies!" (Isaiah 6:3, NLT). The awesome purity of God required sacrifices for sin in order for Israel to approach Him. The ultimate sacrifice was Christ's offering on the cross, so that all who believe could draw near to Him.

Our practice of holiness enables us to commune with God. David the psalmist asked, "Who may worship in your sanctuary, LORD? Who may enter your presence on your holy hill?" The answer is, "Those who lead blameless lives and do what is right" (Psalm 15:1-2, NLT).

God wants us to be holy because purity blesses. Those who desire to live a holy life in this unholy world experience what is good and profitable to the soul. Anytime I play around the edges of the world, the experience ultimately proves to be counterfeit, and afterward I sense that the fleeting moment of pleasure has robbed me of something precious. God loves His children, and He wants us to live in intimacy with Him — and separate from the world — because this will give us the abundant inner life that He promises.

On the night before He was crucified, Jesus told the disciples it was to their advantage that He leave because then, "When He, the Spirit of truth, has come, He will guide you into all truth" (John 16:13, NKJV). It is the *Holy* Spirit who guides and motivates us toward righteousness and obedience. We are not left helpless to keep His commands and to obey God's commands, for He, Himself, says, "I am the Lord who makes you holy." To the Philippians, Paul wrote, "For God is working in you, giving you the desire and the power to do what pleases him" (Philippians 2:13, NLT). Chambers comments, "It is only when we are garrisoned by God with the stupendous sanctity of the Holy Spirit, that spirit, soul, and body are preserved in unspotted integrity, undeserving of censure in God's sight, until Jesus comes."[2] But in order for God to make us holy, we must be willing to set ourselves apart from what is profane and be willing to obey all that is true: "Go out into the world uncorrupted, a breath of fresh air in this squalid and polluted society. Provide people with a glimpse of good living and of the living God" (Philippians 2:15, MSG). And this can only be accomplished as we dwell in His presence.

LISTENING TO THE MOST HIGH

Read Leviticus 20:7-8. What are some common *mis*conceptions of holiness?

EXPERIENCING HIS POWER AND PRESENCE

How are you growing in your understanding of, and desire for, holiness?

Respond in prayer to God's words to you, "Set yourself apart to be holy."

All our endeavors might be unavailing; we might content against the strong current of sin and be baffled and borne along its stream, but if God himself is sanctifying us, we shall prevail. Let us go forth unto the struggle, for we shall assuredly succeed. God sanctifies us in such ways that he acts with us while he acts in us and for us.[3]

— *W. Clarkson*

Dear Father, may I be one of Your set apart ones whose heart is set on pursuing holiness. *Amen.*

I WILL NOT REMEMBER YOUR SINS

I, even I, am He who blots out your transgressions for My
own sake; and I will not remember your sins.

— ISAIAH 43:25, NKJV

I will never forget the first time I drove a car all by myself. I was fourteen years old and had just received my driver's license. My parents had given me permission to pick up some of my girlfriends on the way to a meeting at school. It was exciting, and we were in high spirits. I was careful on the drive in, but on the way home I followed the "directions" of my passengers. I made some unlawful turns and went a little faster than I should have. It seemed fun at the time.

However, after dropping everyone off, I began to feel convicted about my somewhat reckless driving. When I arrived home, I went into my bedroom, knelt down by the bed, and asked God to forgive me for not obeying the law. Even though that was almost fifty years ago and my sin was relatively inconsequential, I still remember the sense of forgiveness I experienced. It was as if the Lord bent down and lifted the burden of guilt from my heart. This was my first experience of knowing that God blots out transgressions.

Through the prophet Isaiah, God recounted His past and future faithfulness to Israel. He brought them out of Egypt, and He would deliver them from Babylonia. He affirmed His loving commitment to them by saying, "You are Mine. When you pass through the waters, I will be with you. . . . Since you were precious in My sight, you have been honored, and I have loved you" (Isaiah 43:1-2,4, NKJV). He reminded them of His power and sovereignty: "Indeed before the day was, I am He; and there is no one who can deliver out of My hand; I work, and who will reverse it?" (verse 13, NKJV). He then rebuked Israel for neglecting Him; they had not sought His guidance or help through prayer: "But you have not called upon Me, O Jacob" (verse 22, NKJV). Ignoring and rejecting a loving parent is cause for reproach. Israel's failure to acknowledge their dependence on the Lord had deteriorated into indifference to Him: "You have been weary of Me, O Israel" (verse 22, NKJV).

This sluggish attitude showed in Israel's laxity in the discipline of making sacrifices — no sheep, no fragrant incense, no honor in their offerings. God could find no excuse for their negligence, because He had not placed burdensome demands on them. As He reviewed Israel's failure to depend upon Him, to rejoice in Him, and to honor Him with appropriate sacrifices, He declared that it was *He* who had grown weary with their faults and was burdened by their sins (verse 24).

If you had a child who continually and willfully refused to obey your reasonable expectations and flouted her ingratitude and disrespect in the face of your consistent and loving parenting, how would you feel? How should the sovereign Lord of creation respond to disobedient, ungrateful children? Matthew Henry commented, "Now one would think it should follow: 'I, even, I, am he that will destroy thee, and burden my self no longer with care about thee.'"[1]

But anger and punishment are not His response. He is a long-suffering God of love. When confronted with His children's sin, He counters with grace: "I — yes, I alone — will blot out your sins for my own sake and will never think of them again" (Isaiah 43:25, NLT). How incredible — God pardons and forgets! In the face of complacency and transgression, the Lord chooses to save and to forgive. And not only that — He blots out our sin. The image here is one of an account book from which the debt is erased. This is a graphic image of God's grace.

This is also the gospel. A few chapters later Isaiah preaches, "All we like sheep have gone astray; we have turned, every one, to his own way; and the LORD has laid on Him the iniquity of us all. . . . And He was numbered with the transgressors, and He bore the sin of many, and made intercession for the transgressors" (Isaiah 53:6,12, NKJV). Paul echoed this prophecy when he wrote to the Romans, "But God showed his great love for us by sending Christ to die for us while we were still sinners" (Romans 5:8, NLT). God forgives for His own name's sake. This is who God is — abounding in love and overflowing in grace. He is a Redeemer and a Restorer. He wants to love His children, and He wants His children to love Him, in holiness and truth. Therefore, He chose to blot out sin through the Atonement — the Cross.

Whosoever believes will not perish, but have everlasting life, declared the apostle John in his gospel (3:16). Acknowledging our sin and need for a Savior grants us forgiveness and eternal life. God pointed to Israel's inability to save themselves when He suggested,

"Let us review the situation together, and you can present your case to prove your innocence" (Isaiah 43:26, NLT). One commentator suggests that this statement is not so much a condemnation as an invitation, meaning: "Remind me of my promises; plead them before me; declare them, that by my free grace I may justify Thee." In humbly pleading before God, Israel had to acknowledge their sin — which, if genuine, would lead to repentance. The commentator continues, "God will not justify the self-righteous. He forgives those only who ask his forgiveness. . . . If we 'go about to establish our own righteousness, and do not submit ourselves to the righteousness of God,' we exclude ourselves from God's covenant of salvation, which is made with the humble, the contrite, the self-abased, the penitent. 'If we confess our sins, he is faithful and just to forgive us our sins' (1 John 1:9)."[2]

To have a God who takes it upon Himself to blot out our sins and never remember them is astounding. How could Israel become weary of Him? How could they neglect to worship Him? But, more important, how can we neglect Him? Why do we forget to call upon Him? Why do we give Him the leftover offerings of our lives? Why do we hesitate to kneel down and ask for the forgiveness He so freely bestows?

The forgiveness I first experienced as a young girl has been extended countless times over the years. Since that time, I have found that God has forgiven far more consequential sins than a teenager's night of driving. How freeing to know that God, who knows all, does not remember our sins. He seeks to restore us and cleanse us, that He might draw us into the secret place of the Most High. He waits only for our response.

LISTENING TO THE MOST HIGH

Read Isaiah 43:25. Using some reference helps, such as a dictionary, a thesaurus, and other Bible versions, write out a few similar phrases for "blots out" and "will not remember." On what basis do we receive the blessing of having our sins blotted out?

EXPERIENCING HIS POWER AND PRESENCE

How does this merciful aspect of God's character encourage you to dwell in His presence? Write about it here or in a private place where you will not worry about anyone other than the Lord seeing it.

Take to the Lord any burdens of guilt or fear that you have been harboring, or any wrong views of Him you have been living with, and ask Him in prayer to cleanse and restore you.

*The great miracle of the grace of God is that He forgives sin,
and it is the death of Jesus Christ alone that enables the Divine
nature to forgive and to remain true to itself in doing so.*[3]

— Oswald Chambers

Dear Father, thank You for Your mercy and grace in not
only forgiving my sins, but in not remembering them. I am
humbled and blessed. *Amen.*

FORGIVE THOSE WHO SIN AGAINST YOU

If you forgive those who sin against you, your heavenly Father will forgive you. But if you refuse to forgive others, your Father will not forgive your sins.

— MATTHEW 6:14-15, NLT

After much instruction and coaxing, one of our children approached his sibling, whom he had insulted, and quietly asked, "Will you forgive me?" I was so pleased to watch this time of reconciliation and to see my child humble himself and ask for forgiveness. The problem that arose next, however, was that there was no response to his request! Apparently, forgiveness was not something the other child wanted to give. Then my instruction and encouragement turned toward helping the offended child understand the importance and necessity of forgiving others.

Forgiveness is a burning passion of God's — a passion that sent His Son all the way to the cross. Because Christ bore the enormous cost of atoning for our sin, God's forgiveness is a free gift to us. We can sing the old hymn, "Jesus paid it all, all to Him I owe; sin had left a crimson stain — He washed it white as snow."[1]

Since God's forgiveness is freely given and undeserved, He simply asks that we do the same. Jesus instructs us to pray in the Lord's Prayer, "Forgive us our sins, as we have forgiven those who sin against us" (Matthew 6:12, NLT). In other words, we are to pray, "Lord, I want You to forgive me in the same way that I forgive others." Just to be sure that we really do grasp God's intense desire that we freely forgive, Jesus further emphasizes the importance of forgiveness by saying: "In prayer there is a connection between what God does and what you do. You can't get forgiveness from God, for instance, without also forgiving others. If you refuse to do your part, you cut yourself off from God's part" (Matthew 6:14-15, MSG).

At first, these seem to be harsh, not loving, words from our Lord. Why is God's forgiveness entwined with how we forgive others? Are these really words of love from the heart of God?

Perhaps the best place to start in answering these questions is by looking at what happens to us when we refuse to forgive another person. Instead of experiencing the freedom of release from this wound, we remain in the bondage of returning to the offense again and again. As we harbor anger and resentment, they keep growing. The devastating harvest of an unforgiving attitude insidiously invades our soul, dominating us from within and destroying any hope of a free and loving spirit.

"A calm and undisturbed mind and heart are the life and health of the body," Proverbs advises, "but envy, jealousy, and wrath are like rottenness of the bones" (14:30, AMP). Our loving Lord wants us to understand that forgiveness is for *us*! What is at stake in our need to pardon others is not essentially their well-being but ours. Often, those who have hurt us are neither repentant nor open to reconciliation. But our forgiveness does not depend upon their response. Rather, it depends upon trusting and obeying the loving words of God: forgive as you have been forgiven. God has paid the cost to forgive us, but if we do not forgive others, then we must bear the consequences of our failure to forgive.

In response to Peter's question of how many times one must forgive, Jesus told the parable of the unforgiving servant. This story pointedly illustrates the extraordinarily forgiving heart of God and the drastic consequences of one who is willing to accept forgiveness but unwilling to give it to others.

The parable begins with a king who is settling his accounts with his officials. One servant, who owes several million dollars, is brought before the king. Of course, he is unable to pay such a vast sum, so the king orders that payment be made by selling him and his family into slavery. Overwhelmed by the weight of the settlement and desperate to save himself and his family, the servant humbles himself and pleads for mercy. The king is so genuinely moved by this entreaty that he compassionately forgives the entire debt.

But that is not the end of the story. This forgiven official no sooner leaves the presence of the king than he runs into one of his fellow servants, who owes him only a few dollars, and demands instant payment of the debt. The indebted servant pleads for patience, but the official shows no mercy and throws his fellow servant into prison.

When word gets back to the king, he summons the official and scolds him: "You evil servant! I forgave you that tremendous debt because you pleaded with me. Shouldn't you have mercy on your fellow servant, just as I had mercy on you?" Then the angry king sends the man to prison to be tortured until he had paid his entire debt. Jesus ends the parable with this sobering truth: "That's what my heavenly Father will do to you if you refuse to forgive your brothers and sisters from your heart" (Matthew 18:35, NLT).

The movie *Dead Man Walking* depicts the last days of Robert Willie, an unrepentant convict who is on death row for raping and killing a young woman. Deborah Morris, who also was kidnapped and raped by Willie but survived the attack, wrote a book about her struggle titled *Forgiving the Dead Man Walking*. She shares, "The refusal to forgive him always meant that I held onto all my Robert Willie–related stuff — my pain, my shame, my self-pity. That's what I gave up in forgiving him. And it wasn't until I did, that real healing could even begin. . . . And even God seems to put a higher priority on forgiveness than on justice. We don't sing *Amazing Justice*, we sing *Amazing Grace*."[2]

Whenever I speak thoughtlessly and hurt others or nurse an offense, God graciously shows me my sin. As I agree with Him about it, He forgives again, and again, and again. He pours out His patience and mercy abundantly on me.

God, who forgives several million dollars, asks us to forgive a few dollars — if we don't, we imprison ourselves. These are strong words from the Most High, but they are loving words, spoken directly to our hearts: may we find the freedom that forgiveness brings as we dwell in His presence and experience His amazing grace.

LISTENING TO THE MOST HIGH

Read Matthew 6:14-15. Why do you think a firsthand experience of God's forgiveness enables someone to let go of nursing wounds and holding grudges?

EXPERIENCING HIS POWER AND PRESENCE

In what areas of your life do you struggle with receiving or giving forgiveness?

Spend some time in prayer, asking God to reveal areas of your heart that have been closed off to His forgiveness or hardened against extending forgiveness to another.

> *The person who accepts forgiveness becomes deeply aware of his own weakness and need. Pride is ruled out as we take our place as supplicants before the Lord. This basic attitude releases us from our tendency to become angry with, or judgmental of, others . . . we are freed to respond as God does, with loving concern and forgiveness. It isn't that God will not forgive the unforgiving. It is simply that the unforgiving lack the humble attitude that both permits them to accept forgiveness and frees them to extend forgiveness.*[3]
>
> *— Lawrence O. Richards*

Dear Lord, the depth of Your love can be measured by the breadth of Your forgiveness. As a forgiven servant of Yours, enable me to forgive from my heart. *Amen.*

GO AND BE RECONCILED

But when your eye is bad, your whole body is filled with darkness. And if the light you think you have is actually darkness, how deep that darkness is! No one can serve two masters. For you will hate one and love the other; you will be devoted to one and despise the other. You cannot serve both God and money.

— MATTHEW 6:23-24, NLT

The other day during my time alone with God, I "suddenly" remembered a recent conversation with a friend. As I recalled my words, I realized that I had not been gracious in speaking about a mutual acquaintance. I called my friend and said, "I need to ask your forgiveness for being unkind toward our friend. I was wrong; will you forgive me?" My friend responded, "Yes, I forgive you and I appreciate the fact that you called." I knew from her response that she felt I had been wrong in what I had said. I needed to be reconciled to her.

This was not a major rift that involved hostility and hurt feelings, but it was sin, and it needed to be dealt with. If I had not acknowledged this to her, there would have been a loss of trust in our friendship. I think it is important to notice that we *remember* our offenses while we are in the act of offering a sacrifice. Offering a sacrifice in biblical times is equivalent to our worshiping God, so when I am before the Lord in an attitude of reverence, the Holy Spirit can speak to my heart. It is then that He can help me remember that someone has something against me.

Jesus is very clear in His teaching about reconciliation. Once a transgression has been brought to our mind, we are to leave our worship and go and be reconciled. It is a high priority with the Lord that we worship with a clear conscience. We cannot go to the Lord and say "I love You" if we are unloving toward others. The Scriptures clearly teach, "If someone says, 'I love God,' and hates his brother, he is a liar; for he who does not love his brother whom he has seen, how can he love God whom he has not seen? And this commandment we have from Him: that he who loves God must love his brother also" (1 John 4:20-21, NKJV).

When we say that we love God, He looks at our heart. He is concerned about the purity of our internal worship. He wants nothing to hinder our relationship to Him — that's why these are words of love. Listen to Psalm 66:18: "If I had not confessed the sin in my heart, the Lord would not have listened" (NLT). Essentially, our worship is blocked until we "unblock" it. We are to go and settle matters — ask forgiveness, make restitution, do whatever we can for reconciliation. Then we can return to our worship in righteousness and freedom.

Jesus' teaching concerning worship is so strong because the people were used to the Pharisees' example. Their worship was all external; they were the personification of hypocrisy! The Lord scathingly rebuked them: "Hypocrites! You are like whitewashed tombs — beautiful on the outside but filled on the inside with dead people's bones and all sorts of impurity. Outwardly you look like righteous people, but inwardly your hearts are filled with hypocrisy and lawlessness" (Matthew 23:27-28, NLT). If we come before God to worship Him and we are unreconciled, then we are like the Pharisees — hypocritical, bound in self-service and self-righteousness. Because God loves us, He clearly instructs us to have pure hearts and unity with one another.

Later in His ministry, Jesus gave instruction on how to respond to someone who has offended us: "If another believer sins against you, go privately and point out the offense" (Matthew 18:15, NLT). In either instance, whether we have sinned or someone has sinned against us, it is our duty to go. A faithful friend, in obedience to this command, brought to my attention a time when I had not been gracious to her. As she explained the circumstances, I realized that in my self-absorption I had not had the sensitivity to see how I had hurt her. I was so thankful that she had come to me so that there would be no barrier in our relationship. Jesus said that when we go and the person listens and confesses, then we have won back a brother. Paul, in his letter to the Romans, wrote, "Do all that you can to live in peace with everyone" (Romans 12:18, NLT). Seeking reconciliation is not a guarantee that the other person will respond. What is important here is doing all that *we* can. Doing our part is all God asks of us. (For teaching on what to do if the other person does not respond, see Matthew 18:16-17).

Samuel reproved King Saul for an act of disobedience after Israel's conquest of the Amalekites. Saul had been instructed to destroy the entire Amalekite nation, including the livestock, but he spared some sheep and cattle and brought them back with him. When Samuel confronted him, Saul tried to defend himself with the excuse that he intended to sacrifice these animals as an offering to God. "What is more pleasing to the LORD," Samuel responded, "your burnt offerings and sacrifices or your obedience to his voice? Listen! Obedience is better than sacrifice" (1 Samuel 15:22, NLT).

We should not deceive ourselves when we are before the Lord. We cannot postpone reconciliation by rationalizing that our time in worship (in whatever form) is more important or that the time is not right. Jesus says to go! It is imperative that we obey, because our relationships with God and others depend on our obedience.

But it is not easy to be reconciled. "Going" involves humbling ourselves, admitting our sin, and making ourselves vulnerable. Once I was convicted of my ungracious remarks, I knew I needed to make the phone call as soon as possible. Otherwise it would be too easy to procrastinate and ultimately justify myself. Perhaps this is why Jesus was so definite about the immediacy of leaving our offering and going to take care of our offense. Jesus also wants us to go, because it is not profitable for us or the body of Christ to be divided and unreconciled.

We have read that the sacrifices that please God are a broken and a contrite heart (Psalm 51:17). Contrition springs from a repentant heart, responding obediently to the conviction of sin — whether brought to our attention by the Lord or through the words of others. Our brokenness and repentance are wonderful antidotes to pride and to the destructive practice of nursing sin in our lives.

Jesus' loving words pose these questions: *Are you reconciled? Do you have a clear conscience before God and man? As much as it depends on you, are you at peace with everyone?* If not, stop now: go and be reconciled!

LISTENING TO THE MOST HIGH

Read Matthew 5:23-24. How might an unreconciled offense, given or received, interfere with a person's relationship with God?

EXPERIENCING HIS POWER AND PRESENCE

What are your greatest struggles with this instruction from the Lord?

Spend some time in quiet prayer, asking God to reveal to you any specific offenses, given or received, for which you need His grace to reconcile.

Jesus does not mention the other person, He says — you go. There is no question of your rights. The stamp of the saint is that he can waive his own rights and obey the Lord Jesus.[1]

— *Oswald Chambers*

Dear Lord, please don't ever let me sin without knowing it. And when I am prompted, please give me the grace to go and be reconciled immediately. *Amen.*

I WILL REPAY THOSE WHO DESERVE IT

Dear friends, never take revenge. Leave that to the righteous anger of God. For the Scriptures say, "I will take revenge; I will pay them back," says the LORD.

— ROMANS 12:19, NLT

While David was the anointed future king of Israel, he experienced a brief respite from the incessant conflict with his jealous, irrational father-in-law, King Saul. This peaceful interlude took place just after the death of the prophet Samuel, when David took his men to the wilderness of Paran.

When supplies ran low, David decided to ask for help from Nabal, a wealthy but surly man who was shearing his sheep in Carmel. Earlier in their journey, David and his men had given some welcome protection to Nabal's shepherds and their flocks. Thinking that Nabal would return a favor, David sent ten of his men to ask for whatever reward Nabal deemed appropriate. Sheepshearing was a festive occasion, and it was customary to share liberally with others at such a time.

Nabal, however, far from being kind and generous, brusquely and disgracefully rejected the men. David was so offended that he assembled four hundred of his warriors and began a march to attack the house of Nabal with the intent of killing him and all his men.

One of Nabal's servants warned Abigail, Nabal's wife, of the impending disaster. She quickly set off to intercept David, sending ahead of her a peace offering — enough food for the entire army on the march. When Abigail met up with David, she humbly pleaded for her husband and household on the basis that perhaps through her intercession, God was keeping David from taking vengeance into his own hands in a manner he would later regret. "When the Lord has done all he promised and has made you leader of Israel, don't let this be a blemish on your record. Then your conscience won't have to bear the staggering burden of needless bloodshed and vengeance" (1 Samuel 25:30-31, NLT).

David graciously accepted Abigail's intervention, and he thanked God for preventing him from taking revenge. When Abigail told her husband the next morning of her meeting with David, Nabal suffered a paralyzing stroke. He lay on his bed, unable to move:

About ten days later, the Lord struck him and he died. When David heard that Nabal was dead, he said, "Praise the Lord, who has avenged the insult I received from Nabal and has kept me from doing it myself. Nabal has received the punishment for his sin." (1 Samuel 25:38-39, NLT)

Why did David praise God for preventing him from taking vengeance on Nabal? Perhaps it is because David knew that had he acted rashly in anger, his revenge would have been much harsher than the slight offense he had suffered. David would have known the Scripture "Do not seek revenge or bear a grudge against a fellow Israelite, but love your neighbor as yourself. I am the LORD" (Leviticus 19:18, NLT). Therefore, he knew his conscience would condemn him if he went ahead with his plan of revenge. God was protecting him from actions he would long regret. Nabal's death confirmed that David could rely on God's fatherly protection. Since God would fight for His children, David did not have to right his own wrongs.

God's promise to repay those who deserve it is a gracious gift of love and freedom for all His children. The Lord takes this responsibility on Himself out of concern for our well-being. Human vengeance is very costly to the avenger. A dictionary definition of *vengeance* is "retribution"; the definition for *avenge* is "to exact satisfaction for a wrong by punishing the wrongdoer." As commentator Albert Barnes indicates, Scripture tells us to leave our wrongs in God's hands: "The command here *not to avenge ourselves* means that we are not to take it out of the hands of God, or the hands of the law, and to inflict it ourselves."[1] We are not created to exact retribution, and we can't carry it out righteously. Only God can repay justly.

When I was in second grade, I confided in my father that I was afraid of some older children at school. I vividly recall my dad telling me that I did not need to worry. If anything ever happened, he would come to my school and protect me. I returned to school armed with the knowledge that my dad would take care of me. He would handle anyone who hurt me. Although nothing occurred, I felt protected and at peace. I was free from worrying about what I might have to do if someone harmed me.

And you have a Father who says lovingly to you, *Because I love you, I don't want you ever to pay back evil for evil. Leave that to Me. I will deal justly with those who hurt you.*

LISTENING TO THE MOST HIGH

Read Romans 12:19. Paul's counsel is illustrated in the story of Abigail, Nabal, and David. Had David not listened to Abigail's plea, he would have had a bloodbath on his conscience. What are some other examples of the cost to us when we take vengeance into our own hands, refusing to trust that God will repay those who deserve it?

EXPERIENCING HIS POWER AND PRESENCE

In what areas of your life are you most likely to try to avenge yourself rather than leaving it to God?

Ask the Lord to search your heart to see if there is any lingering resentment or desire for revenge. Pray for His comfort and assurance in His ability to repay those who deserve it.

Leave it to Me, child; leave it to Me. Dearer thy garden to Me than to thee. Lift up thy heart, child; life up thine eyes; Nought can defeat Me, nought can surprise.

Leave it to Me, child; leave it to Me. Let slip the burden too heavy for thee; That which I will, My Hand shall perform — Fair are the lilies that weather the storm.[2]

— *Amy Carmichael*

Dear Father, only One who loves deeply is willing to vindicate His children. Thank You for this assurance of Your love and protection. *Amen.*

I CORRECT AND DISCIPLINE

I correct and discipline everyone I love.
So be diligent and turn from your indifference.

— REVELATION 3:19, NLT

I was feeling really sorry for myself. I was speaking at a conference, and it seemed that everyone I encountered asked me if I knew a certain speaker. Then they would tell me how much her writing and speaking had meant to them. At this same retreat, the women's ministry director announced an upcoming seminar by this person, and then she praised this dear woman and personally recounted how this author had enriched her life. She informed the group that her women's ministry was going to rent a bus in order to accommodate all the women who were signing up to go.

Through nobody's fault but my own, I began to feel insignificant, useless, and absolutely least in the kingdom of God. My eyes were focused on myself, not on the Lord. My heart was set on my place and position in the kingdom, not on the blessing to the body of Christ of other godly servants who minister and serve. Inwardly I began to withdraw and feel totally inadequate. I was full of *self* and desperately in need of correction.

I heard the Lord's words in my heart: *Cynthia, whose life is it? Haven't you given Me your life to use as I please? Is My love not enough for you? Can you be content with where I want you to be? Can you serve unselfishly and pray for those I am using in more public ways?*

Here was a child who had been corrected and disciplined, but also a child who knew she was loved. Her Father was not going to let her get away with self-pity, with preoccupation about receiving adulation, with comparing herself to someone else. He loved her too much to let her withdraw into selfishness. "The people I love, I call to account — prod and correct and guide so that they'll live at their best" (Revelation 3:19, MSG).

It was with the intent of prodding and correcting that Jesus addressed the church of Laodicea, recorded in Revelation 3. This body of believers was self-satisfied, wealthy, and halfhearted. Jesus pronounced them lukewarm in their faith — a condition that made them distasteful to Him. Spiritual pride can often accompany material prosperity. I recall a story about an artist who was commissioned to create a portrait of an impoverished, struggling church that was limited in its ministry and in need of help. When he finished his work, to the surprise of all those around him, his painting depicted a beautiful, new, expensive church. It looked wealthy from the outside, but it was spiritually poor within. Now, just because a church is well off with attractive facilities does not mean that it is self-absorbed. However, we do know that affluence lulled the Laodiceans into a prideful complacency. Jesus criticized them for saying, "I am rich. I have everything I want. I don't need a thing!" (Revelation 3:17, NLT).

When the Lord painted a true picture of their condition, it was the opposite of how they appeared: "You don't realize that you are wretched and miserable and poor and blind and naked" (3:17, NLT). In His rebuke, He told them how to find genuine wealth:

Buy your gold from me, gold that's been through the refiner's fire. Then you'll be rich. Buy your clothes from me, clothes designed in Heaven. You've gone around half-naked long enough. And buy medicine for your eyes from me so you can see, *really* see. (Revelation 3:18, MSG)

Jesus was the source of all they needed to acquire — all that was eternal, holy, and true.

Humanly speaking, we tend to associate rebuke with shame and rejection. But in His very next breath, Jesus affirmed His love for the Laodiceans: "As many as I love, I rebuke and chasten. Therefore be zealous and repent" (Revelation 3:19, NKJV). He wanted to breathe new life into them, not crush them. How could they change if they were not corrected? How could they repent if they didn't know their sin? How could they become zealous without the Lord's stern words challenging them to do so? This rebuke was evidence of His love.

Solomon recognized our human tendency to misinterpret correction when he counseled his son: "Don't reject the LORD's discipline, and don't be upset when he corrects you. For the LORD corrects those he loves, just as a father corrects a child in whom he delights" (Proverbs 3:11-12, NLT). The writer to the Hebrews cited these proverbs from Solomon, adding that discipline is proof that God is treating us as His own children. If He doesn't discipline us, then we are illegitimate and not really His. The writer continued by describing the great benefits of God's correction:

> But God's discipline is always good for us, so that we might
> share in his holiness. No discipline is enjoyable while it
> is happening — it's painful! But afterward there will be a
> peaceful harvest of right living for those who are trained in
> this way. (Hebrews 12:10-11, NLT)

Sometimes God's correction in our lives takes place through trials. This is the context in which the Hebrews writer was teaching. In the preceding chapter, he described the trials of the faithful, citing Jesus as the ultimate example of enduring hostilities from sinners. As we endure chastening, God is treating us as His children. In persevering through these trials, we share in His holiness. One commentator described it, "To become 'partakers of God's holiness' is to be educated for spending eternity with God."[1]

Whatever way God chooses to correct us, it is always for our eternal good. The Lord's chastening in my life at that conference changed me forever. Before, I had wanted to run away, hide, protect myself from being vulnerable, avoid comparison and embarrassment because I wasn't as good as someone else. Although I had already told the Lord that I only wanted to be His child and to serve Him in any way He wanted, when it came right down to it, I wanted to serve in the way I wanted. This correction was certainly not enjoyable. It was painful! But now, having been trained by it, I have hope of living a quiet harvest of right living before my Lord as I dwell in His secret place.

LISTENING TO THE MOST HIGH

Read Revelation 3:19. How would you explain God's chastening as evidence of His love rather than His displeasure?

EXPERIENCING HIS POWER AND PRESENCE

In what ways do you discern God's correction and discipline in your life?

Spend time in prayer thanking the Lord for loving you enough to correct you when you need it. Ask that you will graciously receive His discipline and as a result will be beautified by His chastisement.

Sorrow accepted as Divine chastisement refines and sanctifies the soul. It stirs its tenderest emotions, and touches its richest chords. It draws the heart towards God himself, as its only Rest and Strength and Joy. The most beautiful human faces are not those which show merely the most regular features and the purest complexion; they are those saintly faces which have been beautified by chastisement — "made perfect through suffering."[2]

— *C. Jerdan*

Dear Lord, thank You for holding me to the highest and best and for faithfully exercising Your divine discipline in my life. *Amen.*

FOLLOW ME

*Then, calling the crowd to join his disciples, he said, "If
any of you wants to be my follower, you must turn from
your selfish ways, take up your cross, and follow me.
If you try to hang on to your life, you will lose it.
But if you give up your life for my sake and for the
sake of the Good News, you will save it."*

— MARK 8:34-35, NLT

The seminar had been advertised and promoted for weeks. In large letters the title read, "Save Your Life — Find Your True Self!" It was to be a free event held in the town park. The speaker or guru, as some called him, had quite a following, and the buzz around town tagged him as a little mystical. He had some faithful disciples, and they had done a good job putting the word out. Some who considered attending thought, *It's free, and the topic is relevant to the new age. If it is not interesting, I can always leave.*

The day of the event, after the crowd had gathered, with little formality the teacher began to speak. "Anyone who intends to come with me has to let me lead," He said. "You're not in the driver's seat; *I* am. Don't run from suffering; embrace it. Follow me and I'll show you how. Self-help is no help at all. Self-sacrifice is the way, my way, to saving yourself, your true self. What good would it do to get everything you want and lose you, the real you? What could you ever trade your soul for?" (Mark 8:34-37, MSG*).

Some left after the first five minutes. "Deny myself? In this world, you have to fight to get anything. How can He say, 'Self-help is no help,' and 'self-sacrifice is the way to save yourself'? What does He know? Not much about human nature and how to survive in this world — that's for sure. And who is He to say He knows about the soul? There's no way I'm going to embrace suffering! I already know my true self, and you only live once, so I'm going for all the world has to offer."

I'm sure that many who heard Jesus say the words in Mark 8:34-35 some two thousand years ago had similar responses. Jesus cut to the heart of the matter when He pronounced the criterion for saving our lives and being His disciples. Logically, His words run counter to what most people, then and now, think of as the good life. These words are not comfortable or easy to put into practice. But they are truth, and they need to be understood and applied.

I memorized these verses many years ago in a translation that reads, "If anyone wishes to come after Me, he must deny himself, and take up his cross daily and follow Me" (Luke 9:23, NASB). The first thing I noticed was that Christ prefaces His "mini" seminar with an "If." Christ does not make us follow Him; it is our choice. He is forthright about the demands of discipleship: it costs the follower initially, but this cost pales in comparison to what is gained eternally. Jesus always wants us to give our voluntary, wholehearted devotion with full knowledge of what He expects.

If we choose to be His disciples, there are three things we must do: *put ourselves aside* — our selfishness in any form — *take up our cross,* and *follow Christ.* Whenever gratification of self collides with what would please Christ, then self must be denied. Recently, I battled putting away selfish ambition. I received a letter detailing all that was being done for a certain person, and I immediately began to envy her accomplishments. I compared myself and began to think that I must fight for publicity, I must help myself! It took a while, but finally the Lord was able to get my attention: *Cynthia, what are you striving for? Why are you seeking recognition? Why do you feel that you must have what someone else has? Can you put aside your selfish ambition? Can you be My disciple who has died to self?*

These were piercing questions that needed to be asked. And it was a humbled child who again had to take up her cross and die to self. I think that taking up my cross means that I am reminded daily to put away selfish ambition. I wish that it could be a once-and-for-all dying, but it is a day-by-day process of shouldering the cross, which prods me to deny myself. Only as I am willing to die to self on a daily basis do I have any motivation to follow Christ. These three facets of discipleship are intertwined.

Jesus reasoned that denying self is essential because in the very act of trying to enrich the self-life, you lose it. It is in surrendering your life to follow Christ that true life is found. I like the way Albert Barnes paraphrased this verse: "He that is anxious to save his *temporal* life, or his comfort and security here, shall lose *eternal* life, or shall fail of heaven. He that is willing to risk or lose his comfort and *life* here for my sake, shall find *life* everlasting, or shall be saved."[1]

The Lord continued by saying, "And what do you benefit if you gain the whole world but lose your own soul? Is anything worth more than your soul?" (Mark 8:36-37, NLT).

How valuable is a human soul? Peter told us,

> For you know that God paid a ransom to save you from
> the empty life you inherited from your ancestors. And the
> ransom he paid was not mere gold or silver. It was the pre-
> cious blood of Christ, the sinless, spotless Lamb of God.
> (1 Peter 1:18-19, NLT)

Our souls are so precious that God purchased them at the sac-
rificial cost of His Son. The worth of the human soul is eternal, for
the soul lives on while the world and all that is temporary pass away.
In essence, Jesus asked, "Why cling to your life to experience only
temporal pleasure when you can give up your life to receive eternal pleasure?" Paul said it well, "Yes, everything else is worthless
when compared with the infinite value of knowing Christ Jesus my
Lord. For his sake I have discarded everything else, counting it all
as garbage, so that I could gain Christ and become one with him"
(Philippians 3:8-9, NLT).

Some people did stay in the park and listen to this Teacher who
taught with authority. They left thinking, *How freeing to get out of
the driver's seat. What a relief not to have to compete, not to be preoc-
cupied with making sure that I get what's coming to me. He taught me
that if I follow Him, He will help me to be free from self and to live for
something far greater and more significant than I could ever experience on my own. I don't want a counterfeit life filled with temporary
gratification; I want a true life filled with all that is eternal from above.
I am choosing to follow Him.*

Are you willing to choose this ancient path of following Christ
by laying aside your selfish ambition and any distractions that will
keep you from dwelling in His presence? In choosing this path that
leads to rest, you will find true life, for the Lord will show you the
way and grant you the joy of His presence and the pleasure of living
with him forever.

LISTENING TO THE MOST HIGH
Read Mark 8:34-35. List some ways in which we try to "keep" our lives.

EXPERIENCING HIS POWER AND PRESENCE
In what ways is God leading you into a deeper experience of losing your life in order to find the life He gives you?

Draw close to the heart of God in prayer, asking Him to teach you how to follow Him more closely.

If the world be gained, nothing is gained; if the soul be lost, everything is lost.[2]

— *A. Rowland*

Dear Lord, help me to embrace Your way of self-sacrifice and surrender so that I may find true life. Thank you for the inexpressible joy and the immeasurable pleasure of dwelling in Your presence. *Amen.*

THE FATHER AND THE CHILD

The Father spoke:

My child, I am pleased that you desire to stay close to Me.

Oh, Father, it is truly the one thing that I seek.

How have you experienced My power and presence?

I realize now that when I dwell in Your secret place, I am able
to sense Your presence more consistently in my day to day
life.

*Only as you dwell in the shelter of the Most High will you truly
come to know of My unfailing love and commitment to
never leave you or forsake you.*

Thank You for being my refuge and fortress. My deepest desire
is to please You and to live according to your Word.

*We have only begun, dear child! Keep My Book open and come
to it with an obedient heart. Continue to come and talk with
Me and let Me guide you along the right path. I love you and
I am delighted that you want to dwell in My presence.*

# NOTES

DAY 1: COME AND TALK WITH ME

1. Andrew Murray, *Abide in Christ* (Springdale, PA: Whitaker House, 1979), 13–14.

DAY 2: WHERE ARE YOU?

1. E. R. Conder and W. Clarkson, *The Pulpit Commentary,* ed. H. D. M. Spence and Joseph S. Excell (Peabody, MA: Hendrickson, n.d.), 8:317.

DAY 3: I STAND AT THE DOOR AND KNOCK

1. A. W. Tozer, *The Pursuit of God* (Camp Hill, PA: Christian Publications, 1982), 82–83.

DAY 4: DON'T BE AFRAID, FOR I AM WITH YOU

1. John McNeill, quoted in Mrs. Charles Cowman, *Words of Comfort and Cheer* (Grand Rapids, MI: Zondervan, 1980), 17 November.
2. George Herbert, quoted in *the New Book of Christian Quotations,* comp. Tony Castle (New York: Crossroad, 1989), 87.

DAY 5: BLESSED ARE THOSE WHO TRUST IN THE LORD

1. W. F. Adeney, *The Pulpit Commentary*, ed. H. D. M. Spence and Joseph S. Excell (Peabody, MA: Hendrickson, n.d.), 9:69.

2. Adeney, 11:420.

DAY 6: I KNOW THE PLANS I HAVE FOR YOU

1. C. S. Lewis, quoted in *The Quotable Lewis*, ed. Wayne Martindale and Jerry Root (Wheaton, IL: Tyndale, 1989), 260.

DAY 7: MY PEACE I GIVE TO YOU

1. B. Thomas, *The Pulpit Commentary*, ed. H. D. M. Spence and Joseph S. Excell (Peabody, MA: Hendrickson, n.d.), 17: vol. 2, 258.

2. J. R. Thomson, *The Pulpit Commentary*, 17: vol. 2, 247.

DAY 8: I HAVE OVERCOME THE WORLD

1. *The Bible Knowledge Commentary*, ed. John F. Walvoord and Roy B. Zuck (Wheaton, IL: Victor, 1983), 330.

2. B. Thomas, *The Pulpit Commentary*, ed. H. D. M. Spence and Joseph S. Excell (Peabody, MA: Hendrickson, n.d.), 17: vol. 2, 332.

DAY 9: STORE YOUR TREASURES IN HEAVEN

1. P. C. Barker, in *The Pulpit Commentary*, ed. H. D. M. Spence and Joseph S. Excell (Peabody, MA: Hendrickson, n.d.), 15:259.

2. Charles H. Spurgeon, *Morning and Evening*, ed. Roy H. Clarke (Nashville: Thomas Nelson, 1994), 11 May.

DAY 10: I AM THE FIRST AND THE LAST

1. William Ullathorne, quoted in *The Matthew Henry Commentary on the Whole Bible* (Iowa Falls: Riverside, n.d.), 5:684.

Day 11: BUT ON THIS ONE I WILL LOOK

1. A. W. Tozer, *The Pursuit of God* (Camp Hill, PA: Christian Publications, 1982), 113.
2. Nicholas Cusa, quoted in Tozer, *Pursuit of God*, 92.

Day 12: YOUR NAMES ARE WRITTEN IN HEAVEN

1. Matthew Henry, *The Matthew Henry Commentary on the Whole Bible* (Iowa Falls: Riverside, n.d.), 5:684.

Day 13: SHUT THE DOOR

1. David M'Intyre, *The Hidden Life of Prayer* (Minneapolis: Bethany House, 1993), 29.

Day 14: ABIDE IN MY WORD

1. Oswald Chambers, *My Utmost for His Highest* (Westwood, NJ: Barbour & Co., 1935), 10 October.
2. Andrew Murray, *Abide in Christ* (Springdale, PA: Whitaker House, 1979), 8.

Day 15: THE TRUTH WILL SET YOU FREE

1. Matthew Henry, *The Matthew Henry Commentary on the Whole Bible* (Iowa Falls: Riverside, n.d.), 5:994.
2. Henry, 5:995.

Day 16: KEEP MY COMMANDMENTS

1. Albert Barnes, *Notes on the New Testament* (Grand Rapids, MI: Baker, 1998), vol. 9: 339.
2. B. Thomas, *The Pulpit Commentary*, ed. H. D. M. Spence and Joseph S. Excell (Peabody, MA: Hendrickson, n.d.), 17: vol. 2, 252.

DAY 17: HE WILL GIVE YOU ANOTHER COUNSELOR

1. Martyn Lloyd-Jones, *God the Holy Spirit* (Wheaton, IL: Crossway, 1997), 17.
2. Lloyd-Jones, 21.

DAY 18: BUT BY MY SPIRIT

1. D. Thomas, *The Pulpit Commentary*, ed. H. D. M. Spence and Joseph S. Excell (Peabody, MA: Hendrickson, n.d.), 14:47.

DAY 19: LOOK FOR THE ANCIENT PATHS

1. S. Conway, *The Pulpit Commentary*, ed. H. D. M. Spence and Joseph S. Excell (Peabody, MA: Hendrickson, n.d.), 11:172; 173.
2. C. S. Lewis, *God in the Dock* (Grand Rapids, MI: Eerdmans, 1970), 201.
3. J. Waite, *The Pulpit Commentary*, 11:177.

DAY 20: KEEP THEM FROM THE EVIL ONE

1. B. Thomas, *The Pulpit Commentary*, ed. H. D. M. Spence and Joseph S. Excell (Peabody, MA: Hendrickson, n.d.), 17: vol., 369.

DAY 21: FEAR ONLY GOD

1. From a newsletter produced by Global Chinese Ministries (Littleton, CO: OMF International), November 2000.
2. Matthew Henry, *The Matthew Henry Commentary on the Whole Bible* (Iowa Falls: Riverside, n.d.), 5:141.
3. B. C. Caffin, *The Pulpit Commentary*, ed. H. D. M. Spence and Joseph S. Excell (Peabody, MA: Hendrickson, n.d.), 15:423.

DAY 22: DO NOT FEAR THE REPROACH OF MEN

1. Matthew Henry, *The Matthew Henry Commentary on the Whole Bible* (Iowa Falls: Riverside, n.d.), 4:290.

2. Amy Carmichael, *If* (Grand Rapids, MI: Zondervan, 1972).

DAY 23: LOVE ME MORE THAN . . .

1. Matthew Henry, *The Matthew Henry Commentary on the Whole Bible* (Iowa Falls: Riverside, n.d.), 5:737.

2. Amy Carmichael, *Whispers of His Power* (Old Tappan, NJ: Fleming H. Revell, 1982), 158.

DAY 24: SET YOURSELVES APART TO BE HOLY

1. Oswald Chambers, *My Utmost for His Highest* (Westwood, NJ: Barbour & Co., 1935), 27 December.

2. Chambers, 9 January.

3. W. Clarkson, *The Pulpit Commentary*, ed. H. D. M. Spence and Joseph S. Excell (Peabody, MA: Hendrickson, n.d.), 2:317.

DAY 25: I WILL NOT REMEMBER YOUR SINS

1. Matthew Henry, *The Matthew Henry Commentary on the Whole Bible* (Iowa Falls: Riverside, n.d.), 4:240.

2. Henry, 4:240.

3. Oswald Chambers, *My Utmost for His Highest* (Westwood, NJ: Barbour & Co., 1935), 19 November.

DAY 26: FORGIVE THOSE WHO SIN AGAINST YOU

1. Elvina M. Hall, "Jesus Paid It All," in *Hymns for the Family of God* (Nashville: Paragon Associates, 1976), 273.

2. Deborah Morris, quoted in Cathy Grossman, "Forgiving the Dead Man Walking," *USA Today*, 12 November 1998.

3. Lawrence O. Richards, *Expository Dictionary of Bible Words* (Grand Rapids, MI: Zondervan, 1985), 291.

DAY 27: GO AND BE RECONCILED

1. Oswald Chambers, *My Utmost for His Highest* (Westwood, NJ: Barbour & Co., 1935), 26 September.

DAY 28: I WILL REPAY THOSE WHO DESERVE IT

1. Albert Barnes, *Notes on the New Testament* (Grand Rapids, MI: Baker, 1998), 10:282.
2. Amy Carmichael, *Mountain Breezes, The Collected Poems of Amy Carmichael* (Fort Washington, PA: Christian Literature Crusade, 1999), 334.

DAY 29: I CORRECT AND DISCIPLINE

1. C. Jerdan, *The Pulpit Commentary*, ed. H. D. M. Spence and Joseph S. Excell (Peabody, MA: Hendrickson, n.d.), 21:366.
2. Jerdan, 21:366.

DAY 30: FOLLOW ME

1. Albert Barnes, *Notes on the New Testament* (Grand Rapids, MI: Baker, 1998), 9:115–116.
2. A. Rowland, *The Pulpit Commentary*, ed. H. D. M. Spence and Joseph S. Excell (Peabody, MA: Hendrickson, n.d.), 16:353.

ABOUT THE AUTHOR

CYNTHIA HEALD was born in Houston, Texas, and received Christ as her personal Savior when she was twelve years old. In 1960, Cynthia married Jack, who by profession is a veterinarian but has been on staff with The Navigators since 1978. They have lived in Tucson, Arizona, since 1977. They are the parents of four (two daughters and two sons) and grandparents of nine.

Cynthia is the author of *Becoming a Women of Excellence, Intimacy with God, Loving Your Husband, Becoming a Woman of Freedom, Becoming a Woman of Purpose, Becoming a Woman of Prayer, Becoming a Woman Who Walks with God, A Woman's Journey to the Heart of God, Becoming a Woman of Grace, When the Father Holds You Close, Becoming a Woman of Faith, Becoming a Woman Who Loves, Maybe God Is Right After All*, and *Uncommon Beauty*.

Cynthia speaks frequently for women's retreats and seminars nationally and internationally. She loves to share the Word of God, be with her husband and family, take bubble baths, have tea parties, and eat out.

Rediscover a classic with Cynthia Heald!

Becoming a Woman Who Loves
Cynthia Heald
978-1-61521-023-7

In *Becoming a Woman Who Loves*, Cynthia Heald takes you by the hand to explore the incredible nature of Christlike love and how God empowers us to love as Jesus loved.

Becoming a Woman of Faith
Cynthia Heald

978-1-61521-021-3

In this inspiring Bible study, best-selling Bible teacher Cynthia Heald offers a realistic, practical perspective for today's Christian woman. *Becoming a Woman of Faith* will strengthen and encourage you as Cynthia shares candidly from her own faith journey. You'll see yourself in her personal struggles to walk in faith and trust and grow from her special insights from God's Word.

Becoming a Woman of Grace
Cynthia Heald

978-1-61521-022-0

Cynthia Heald guides you on a life-transforming journey into the boundless riches of God's grace. Together you will explore the many ways in which God's grace enriches your Christian walk, how to know His grace more fully, and how to extend His grace to others, moment by moment and day by day.